Joseph Deharbe

A catechism of the Catholic Religion

Joseph Deharbe

A catechism of the Catholic Religion

ISBN/EAN: 9783742857439

Manufactured in Europe, USA, Canada, Australia, Japa

Cover: Foto ©Lupo / pixelio.de

Manufactured and distributed by brebook publishing software (www.brebook.com)

Joseph Deharbe

A catechism of the Catholic Religion

A CATECHISM

OF THE

CATHOLIC RELIGION.

TRANSLATED FROM THE GERMAN
OF
THE REV. JOSEPH DEHARBE, S.J.

PRECEDED BY
A SHORT HISTORY OF RELIGION.

EDITED BY THE
RIGHT REV. P. N. LYNCH, D.D.,
BISHOP OF CHARLESTON.

NEW EDITION.

NEW YORK:
THE CATHOLIC PUBLICATION SOCIETY CO.,
9 BARCLAY STREET.

1889.

Imprimatur.

NEW YORK, SEPTEMBER 7, 1878.

CONTENTS.

	PAGE
DAILY DEVOTIONS,	5

A SHORT HISTORY OF RELIGION.

BEFORE CHRIST,	17
HISTORY OF CHRIST,	24
AFTER CHRIST,	28
CONCLUDING REMARKS,	44

INTRODUCTION.

ON THE END OF MAN,	49

PART I.

On Faith.

MEANING, OBJECT, AND RULE OF FAITH,	51
NECESSITY OF FAITH,	53
QUALITIES OF FAITH,	54

On the Apostles' Creed.

FIRST ARTICLE,	56
On God and His Attributes and Perfections,	56
On the Three Divine Persons,	60
On the Creation and Government of the World,	61
On the Angels,	63
On our First Parents and their Fall,	65
SECOND ARTICLE,	67
Jesus Christ the Promised Messias,	67
Jesus Christ, True God,	68
THIRD ARTICLE,	69
The Incarnation of Christ,	69
The Youth of Jesus,	71
The Public Life of Jesus,	72
FOURTH ARTICLE,	73
FIFTH ARTICLE,	74
SIXTH ARTICLE,	76
SEVENTH ARTICLE,	76
EIGHTH ARTICLE,	78
NINTH ARTICLE,	79
The Marks of the Church,	82
The Qualities of the Church,	83
The Growth and Preservation of the Church,	85
The Communion of Saints,	87
TENTH ARTICLE,	88
ELEVENTH ARTICLE,	89
TWELFTH ARTICLE,	90

Contents.

PART II.

The Commandments.

	PAGE
THE CHIEF COMMANDMENT.	92
The Love of God,	92
The Love of our Neighbor,	94
Christian Self-Love,	96
THE TEN COMMANDMENTS OF GOD,	97
First Commandment of God,	98
The Veneration and Invocation of Saints,	100
Second Commandment of God,	102
Third Commandment of God,	104
Fourth Commandment of God,	105
Fifth Commandment of God,	107
Sixth Commandment of God,	109
Seventh Commandment of God,	110
Eighth Commandment of God,	112
Ninth and Tenth Commandments of God,	114
THE SIX COMMANDMENTS OF THE CHURCH,	115
First Commandment of the Church,	116
Second Commandment of the Church,	117
Third, Fourth, and Fifth Commandments of the Church,	119
Sixth Commandment of the Church,	120
ON THE VIOLATION OF THE COMMANDMENTS,	120
On Sin in general,	120
On the different kinds of Sin,	122
ON VIRTUE AND CHRISTIAN PERFECTION,	125
On Virtue,	125
On Christian Perfection,	128

PART III.

On the Means of Grace.

GRACE IN GENERAL,	131
On the Grace of Assistance,	131
The Grace of Sanctification,	132
THE SACRAMENTS,	134
Baptism,	136
Confirmation,	139
The Holy Eucharist,	141
The Real Presence of Christ in the Blessed Sacrament,	141
The Holy Sacrifice of the Mass,	144
Holy Communion,	147
Penance,	150
Examination of Conscience,	152
Contrition,	155
Confession,	157
Satisfaction,	160
Indulgences,	161
Extreme Unction,	162
Holy Orders,	163
Matrimony,	165
SACRAMENTALS,	167
PRAYER,	168
The Angelic Salutation,	173
The Lord's Prayer,	171
RELIGIOUS PRACTICES AND CEREMONIES,	174
RECAPITULATION,	177
Our Religion is Divine,	177

DAILY DEVOTIONS.

THE SIGN OF THE CROSS.

In nomine Patris, et Filii, et Spiritus Sancti. Amen.

In the name of the Father, and of the Son, and of the Holy Ghost. Amen.

THE LORD'S PRAYER.

Pater noster, qui es in cœlis, sanctificetur nomen tuum; adveniat regnum tuum; fiat voluntas tua, sicut in cœlo et in terra. Panem nostrum quotidianum da nobis hodie. Et dimitte nobis debita nostra, sicut et nos dimittimus debitoribus nostris. Et ne nos inducas in tentationem; sed libera nos a malo. Amen.

Our Father, who art in heaven, hallowed be thy name; thy kingdom come; thy will be done on earth as it is in heaven. Give us this day our daily bread. And forgive us our trespasses as we forgive them that trespass against us. And lead us not into temptation; but deliver us from evil. Amen.

THE ANGELICAL SALUTATION.

Ave Maria, gratia plena; Dominus tecum; benedicta tu in mulieribus, et benedictus fructus ventris tui, Jesus. Sancta Maria, Mater Dei, ora pro nobis peccatoribus, nunc

Hail, Mary, full of grace, the Lord is with thee; blessed art thou among women, and blessed is the fruit of thy womb, Jesus. Holy Mary, Mother of God, pray for us sinners,

et in hora mortis nostræ. Amen.

now, and at the hour of our death. Amen.

THE APOSTLES' CREED.

Credo in Deum, Patrem omnipotentem, Creatorem cœli et terræ. Et in Jesum Christum, Filium ejus unicum, Dominum nostrum; qui conceptus est de Spiritu Sancto, natus ex Maria Virgine, passus sub Pontio Pilato, crucifixus, mortuus, et sepultus; descendit ad inferos; tertia die resurrexit a mortuis; ascendit ad cœlos, sedet ad dexteram Dei Patris omnipotentis; inde venturus est judicare vivos et mortuos. Credo in Spiritum Sanctum, sanctam Ecclesiam Catholicam, Sanctorum communionem, remissionem peccatorum, carnis resurrectionem, vitam æternam. Amen.

I believe in God the Father Almighty, Creator of heaven and earth. And in Jesus Christ, his only Son, our Lord, who was conceived by the Holy Ghost, born of the Virgin Mary, suffered under Pontius Pilate, was crucified, dead, and buried; he descended into hell; the third day he rose again from the dead; he ascended into heaven, and sitteth at the right hand of God the Father Almighty; from thence he shall come to judge the living and the dead. I believe in the Holy Ghost, the holy Catholic Church, the communion of saints, the forgiveness of sins, the resurrection of the body, and life everlasting. Amen.

GLORIA PATRI.

Gloria Patri, et Filio, et Spiritui Sancto. Sicut

Glory be to the Father, and to the Son, and to the

erat in principio, et nunc, et semper, et in sæcula sæculorum. Amen.

Holy Ghost. As it was in the beginning, is now, and ever shall be, world without end. Amen.

THE CONFITEOR.

Confiteor Deo omnipotenti, beatæ Mariæ semper virgini, beato Michaeli archangelo, beato Joanni Baptistæ, sanctis apostolis Petro et Paulo, et omnibus sanctis, quia peccavi nimis, cogitatione, verbo, et opere, mea culpa, mea culpa, mea maxima culpa. Ideo precor beatam Mariam semper virginem, beatum Michaelem archangelum, beatum Joannem Baptistam, sanctos apostolos Petrum et Paulum, et omnes sanctos, orare pro me ad Dominum Deum nostrum.

I confess to Almighty God, to blessed Mary ever virgin, to blessed Michael the Archangel, to blessed John the Baptist, to the holy Apostles Peter and Paul, and to all the saints, that I have sinned exceedingly in thought, word, and deed, through my fault, through my fault, through my most grievous fault. Therefore I beseech the blessed Mary ever virgin, the blessed Michael the Archangel, the blessed John the Baptist, the holy Apostles Peter and Paul, and all the saints, to pray to the Lord our God for me.

Misereatur mei omnipotens Deus, et dimissis peccatis meis, perducat me ad vitam æternam. Amen.

May the Almighty God have mercy on me, forgive me my sins, and bring me to everlasting life. Amen.

Indulgentiam, absolutionem, et remissionem

May the Almighty and merciful Lord grant me

peccatorum meorum, tribuat mihi omnipotens et misericors Dominus. Amen.

pardon, absolution, and remission of my sins. Amen.

SALVE REGINA.

Salve, Regina, Mater misericordiæ;
Vita, dulcedo, et spes nostra, salve.
Ad te clamamus, exules filii Hevæ;
Ad te suspiramus, gementes et flentes in hac lacrymarum valle.
Eia ergo, Advocata nostra,
Illos tuos misericordes oculos ad nos converte;
Et Jesum, benedictum fructum ventris tui,
Nobis post hoc exilium ostende.
O clemens, O pia, O dulcis Virgo Maria.
V. Ora pro nobis, sancta Dei Genitrix.
R. Ut digni efficiamur promissionibus Christi.

Hail, Queen, Mother of mercy;
Our life, our sweetness, and our hope, hail.
To thee we cry, poor exiled sons of Eve;
To thee we sigh, weeping and mourning in this vale of tears.
O therefore, our Advocate,
Turn upon us those merciful eyes of thine;
And show us, after this our exile,
The blessed fruit of thy womb, Jesus.
O merciful, O kind, O sweet Virgin Mary!
V. Pray for us, O holy Mother of God.
R. That we may be made worthy of the promises of Christ.

MEMORARE.

Memorare, O piissima Virgo Maria, non esse au-

Remember, O most gracious Virgin Mary, that

ditum a sæculo, quemquam ad tua currentem præsidia, tua implorantem auxilia, tua petentem suffragia, esse derelictum. Ego, tali animatus confidentia, ad te, Virgo virginum, Mater, curro; ad te venio; coram te gemens peccator assisto. Noli, Mater Verbi, verba mea despicere, sed audi propitia et exaudi. Amen.

never was it known that any one who fled to thy protection, implored thy help, and sought thy intercession was left unaided. Inspired with this confidence, I fly unto thee, O Virgin of virgins, my Mother. To thee I come; before thee I stand, sinful and sorrowful. O Mother of the Word Incarnate! despise not my petitions, but in thy mercy hear and answer me. Amen.

THE ANGELUS.

In Paschal time, instead of the Angelus, the Regina Cœli is said standing.

I. *V.* Angelus Domini nuntiavit Mariæ.
R. Et concepit de Spiritu Sancto.
Ave Maria, etc.
II. *V.* Ecce ancilla Domini.
R. Fiat mihi secundum verbum tuum.
Ave Maria, etc.
III. *V.* Et Verbum caro factum est.
R. Et habitavit in nobis.
Ave Maria, etc.
V. Ora pro nobis, Sancta Dei Genitrix.
R. Ut digni efficiamur promissionibus Christi.

I. The angel of the Lord announced unto Mary.
R. And she conceived of the Holy Ghost.
Hail Mary, etc.
II. Behold the handmaid of the Lord.
R. Be it done unto me according to thy word.
Hail Mary, etc.
III. And the Word was made flesh.
R. And dwelt among us.
Hail Mary, etc.
V. Pray for us, O Holy Mother of God!
R. That we may be made worthy of the promises of Christ.

Oremus.	Let us pray.
Gratiam tuam, quæsumus, Domine, mentibus nostris infunde; ut qui, angelo nuntiante, Christi filii tui incarnationem cognovimus, per passionem ejus et crucem ad resurrectionis gloriam perducamur; per eundem Christum Dominum nostrum. Amen.	Pour forth, we beseech thee, O Lord, thy grace into our hearts, that we, to whom the incarnation of Christ thy Son was made known by the message of an angel, may by his passion and cross be brought to the glory of his resurrection; through the same Christ our Lord. Amen.

MORNING PRAYERS.

As soon as you awake make the sign ✚ of the cross and say:

GLORY be to the Father, who has created me. Glory be to the Son, who has redeemed me. Glory be to the Holy Ghost, who has sanctified me. Blessed be the holy and undivided Trinity now and for ever. Amen.

On rising from your bed say:

IN the name of our Lord Jesus Christ, I arise. May he bless, preserve, and govern me, and bring me to everlasting life. Amen.

When dressed, kneel and say:

IN the name of the ✚ Father, and of the Son, and of the Holy Ghost. Amen.

AN ACT OF ADORATION.

O GREAT God, the Sovereign Lord of heaven and earth, I prostrate myself before thee. With all the angels and saints I adore thee. I acknowledge thee to be my Creator and Lord, my first beginning and last end. I give thee homage for my being and life. I submit to thy holy will; and I devote myself to thy divine service this day and for ever.

AN ACT OF FAITH.

O MY God! I firmly believe all the sacred truths which thy holy Catholic Church believes and teaches; because thou hast revealed them, who canst neither deceive nor be deceived.

AN ACT OF HOPE.

O MY God! relying on thy infinite goodness and promises, I hope to obtain the pardon of my sins, the assistance of thy grace, and life everlasting, through the merits of Jesus Christ, our Lord and Saviour.

AN ACT OF LOVE.

O MY God! I love thee above all things, with my whole heart and soul, purely because thou art infinitely perfect and deserving of all love. I love also my neighbor as myself for the love of thee. I forgive all who have injured me, and I ask pardon of all whom I have injured.

AN ACT OF THANKSGIVING.

O GLORIOUS Trinity! I praise thee and give thee thanks for the numberless benefits thou hast bestowed upon me. I thank thee, O heavenly Father! for having created me to thy own image and likeness, and for having preserved me to this day. I thank thee, O merciful Son! for having redeemed me by thy death, and so often fed me with thy precious body and blood. I thank thee, O Holy Spirit! for having cleansed my soul by thy grace in baptism, for having called me into thy Church, and so often washed me from my sins in the sacrament of penance. I thank thee, O most bountiful God! for preserving me during the past night, and granting me this day to serve thee. What return, O my God, can I make to thee for all thou hast done for me? I will bless thy holy name, and serve thee all the days of my life. Bless the Lord, O my soul! let all that is within me praise his holy name.

Here call to mind the sins you are most given to, and resolve to avoid them and all other sins during the day.

AN ACT OF CONTRITION.

MY conscience, O Lord! still reproaches me for my weakness and unfaithfulness. I am heartily sorry for having offended thy infinite goodness. I firmly resolve to avoid sin for the future, and, with the help of thy grace, to die rather than offend thee again.

Make a firm resolution to avoid evil and to do good.

ADORABLE Jesus! Divine model of that perfection for which we should all strive! this day I shall try to imitate thee; to be mild, chaste, zealous, patient, charitable, and resigned. Incline my heart to keep thy commandments. I am resolved to watch over myself with the greatest care, and to live soberly, justly, and piously for the time to come. I will be careful of my ways, that I may not offend with my tongue. I will turn away my eyes, that they may not see vanity; and I will be particularly watchful not to fall back this day into any of my usual errors, but will struggle against them with thy gracious assistance. Enlighten my mind, purify my heart, and guide my steps, that I may pass all my life in thy service. Amen.

Here say the Lord's Prayer, Hail Mary, the Apostles' Creed, the Confiteor, and the Memorare, pp. 5–8.

GRACE BEFORE MEAT.

V. Benedic, Domine, nos et hæc tua dona, quæ de tua largitate sumus sumpturi; per Christum Dominum nostrum. *R.* Amen.

V. Bless us, O Lord, and these thy gifts which of thy bounty we are about to receive; through Christ our Lord. *R.* Amen.

GRACE AFTER MEAT.

V. Agimus tibi gratias, omnipotens Deus, pro universis beneficiis tuis; qui vivis et regnas in sæcula sæculorum. *R.* Amen.

V. We give thee thanks, Almighty God, for all thy benefits; who livest and reignest, world without end. *R.* Amen.

NIGHT PRAYERS.

In the name of the Father, and of the Son, and of the Holy Ghost. Amen.

Blessed be the holy and undivided Trinity, now and for ever. Amen.

Come, O Holy Ghost! fill the hearts of thy faithful, and kindle in them the fire of thy love.

Place yourself in the presence of God.

GREAT God, Lord of heaven and earth! I prostrate myself before thee. With all the angels and saints I adore thee. I acknowledge thee to be my Creator and sovereign Lord, my first beginning and last end. I make thee homage for my being and life. I submit myself to thy holy will; and I devote myself to thy service, now and for ever. Amen.

AN ACT OF FAITH.

Here repeat Faith, Hope, and Love, as on page 11.

Give thanks.

HOW shall I be able to thank thee, O Lord! for all thy favors. Thou hast thought of me from all eternity; thou hast brought me forth from nothing; thou hast given thy life to redeem me, and thou continuest daily to load me with thy favors. Alas! my God, what return can I make thee for all thy benefits, and, in particular, for the favors of this day? Join with me, ye blessed spirits and all ye elect, in praising the God of mercies, who is so good to so unworthy a creature.

Ask for light to discover your sins.

O HOLY GHOST! Eternal source of light! remove my darkness, and drive away those shades that keep me from seeing the enormity of my offences. Show me, I beseech thee, the sins I have committed this day in thought, word, and action. Grant that I may detest them all from the bottom of my heart, and that I may fear nothing so much as ever to commit them again.

Examine your conscience. Consider where you have been this day, and in what company. Call to mind the duties of your state, and your different offences.

Against God.—By omission or negligence in our religious duties; irreverence in the church or wilful distractions in prayer; resistance to the divine grace; oaths; murmurings; want of confidence and resignation.

Against our neighbor.—By rash judgments; hatred; jealousy; contempt; desire of revenge; quarrelling; passion; imprecations; injuries; detraction; raillery; false reports; damaging either in goods or reputation; bad example; scandal; want of obedience, respect, charity, or fidelity.

Against ourselves.—By vanity; human respect; lies; thoughts, desires, discourses, or actions contrary to purity; intemperance; rage or impatience; an useless and sensual life; sloth in not complying with the duties of our state.

Say the Confiteor, as on p. 7.

AN ACT OF CONTRITION.

BEHOLD me, O Lord! overwhelmed with confusion; look upon me, a miserable sinner, according to the multitude of thy mercies. I acknowledge and confess, and am heartily sorry for, all the sins of my past life, and of this day in particular. I cast myself at thy feet, and beseech thee to cover all my sins with that infinite love with which thou hast loved us from all eternity. I grieve from the bottom of my heart that I have been so ungrateful to thee for thy benefits, and have so often offended thee, my God and my chief good. Spare me, I beseech thee, by the death and love of Jesus Christ thy Son; and mercifully forgive whatsoever sins I have this day, or heretofore, committed against thee, my neighbor, or myself.

Make a firm purpose of amendment.

O ETERNAL God! against whom I have sinned, I wish from my heart I had never offended thee; but as I have been so unhappy, oh! grant me now the grace never more to offend thee. Thou willest not the death of a sinner, but rather that he be converted and live. Convert me, then, and I shall be converted. Have mercy on me according to thy great mercy, and according to the multitude of thy mercies blot out my iniquities. I renounce all sin, and firmly purpose to shun all the occasions of it, and to walk henceforth in the path of thy commandments. This is my fixed resolution, which I hope I shall faithfully keep, relying upon thy help; through Jesus Christ our Lord. Amen.

On going to bed say:

✠ In the name of our Lord Jesus Christ crucified, I lay me down to rest; may he bless, govern, and preserve me, and bring me to everlasting life. Amen.

A SHORT HISTORY OF RELIGION.

BEFORE CHRIST.

FROM ADAM TO MOSES.

1. In the beginning God created heaven and earth. He said, "Let them be made," and they were made. He made the whole world—the sun, moon, and stars, the plants and animals, and, last of all, He made man after His own image and likeness. The first man was called Adam, and the first woman Eve. They were good and happy, and dwelt in a pleasant land called the Garden of Eden, or Paradise, and they and their descendants were never to die (4004 B.C.)

2. God forbade Adam and Eve to eat of the Tree of Knowledge which stood in the middle of Eden. But the serpent tempted them, saying: "If you eat thereof, you shall be as Gods," and they believed the serpent and disobeyed God. For this sin of disobedience they were immediately punished, and the punishment fell also upon all their descendants. Adam and Eve were driven out of Paradise; they were doomed to suffering and death, and to be shut out from the presence of God for ever. Yet God took pity on them and promised them a *Saviour*, who should reconcile them again to him, and, if they

---

1. When did God create man? How did He create heaven and earth? How did He distinguish man from the other creatures? What were the names of the first man and woman? Where did they live? Were they and their children ever to die?

2. What commandment did God give to Adam and Eve? What did the serpent tell them? What did Adam and Eve do? Were they punished for it? Were they alone punished? What punishment came

did penance, would make them partakers of eternal happiness in heaven (Gen. iii. 15).

3. Our first parents' sons, Cain and Abel, offered sacrifice to God, and God was pleased with the virtuous Abel's sacrifice, but not with the wicked Cain's. Cain, being jealous and very angry at this, killed his brother (3876 B.C.) For this horrible crime God cursed Cain, who then became a wanderer on the earth.

4. Many of Cain's descendants also were wicked, and in time so seduced the good that men turned away from God and sank deep in sin and vice. For this God destroyed the race of Adam by a deluge. The rain fell for forty days and forty nights, and the waters rose above the highest mountains. Every living creature perished in the flood, except Noe and his family and the animals he had taken into the ark which God had commanded him to build (2348 B.C.) When the flood was over Noe offered a sacrifice of thanksgiving to the Lord for his escape, and the Lord promised Noe that "there should no more be waters of a flood, to destroy all flesh" (Gen. ix. 15).

5. Noe's descendants became so numerous that they began to spread into many lands. But before separating they undertook to build a tower that should reach up to heaven. God, however, confused their language, and, as they could no longer understand one another, they were compelled to stop the

---

upon them? Did God then abandon them? What did He promise them?

3. Who were Cain and Abel? How did they worship God? Was God pleased with their sacrifices? What did Cain do, and what became of him?

4. Were the descendants of Cain good or wicked? What evil did they do? What did God then resolve to do? How long did it rain? To what height did the flood rise? Did all living creatures perish? What did Noe do when he came out of the ark? What new kindness did God show to Noe and his sons?

5. Did the descendants of Noe multiply much? What did they attempt to do? How was their undertaking frustrated? What was the tower called? Did the descendants of Noe remain faithful to God?

work, and the tower was called the *Tower of Babel,* or *Confusion.* Very many of Noe's descendants, instead of adoring the true God, worshipped the sun and the stars, men and animals, and even idols or images.

6. But Abraham kept the true faith and a hope in the Redeemer to come. God made a covenant with him and promised him that the *Messias* should be born of his posterity (1921 B.C.) God distinguished Abraham and his descendants—who were called *Hebrews,* and afterwards *Israelites,* or *Jews*—from other nations, and He often revealed Himself to them.

7. To try Abraham's faith God commanded him to offer up his only son, Isaac, in sacrifice on Mount Moriah. Abraham loaded his son with the wood for the sacrifice, and the two ascended the mountain. But when Isaac had willingly laid himself upon the wood to be offered up, God, through an angel, saved him and blessed Abraham for his obedience (1896 B.C.)

8. Isaac had a son, the patriarch Jacob, who dwelt with his family in the land of Chanaan. Jacob, who was also called Israel, had twelve sons, and these became the fathers of the twelve tribes of Israel. One of these sons, who was called Joseph, was sold by his brothers (1723 B.C.) to some Ismaelite merchants, by whom he was carried into Egypt, where he was falsely accused and thrown into prison. Upon regaining his liberty the king made him chief ruler over all Egypt; and as he, by his wisdom, saved the country from a dreadful famine, he was called "the

---

6. Were the true religion and the hope in the Redeemer entirely to vanish? How did God prevent it? How were the descendants of Abraham called? What favor did God bestow on them?

7. How did God try the faith of Abraham? How did he fulfil the command of God? What did Isaac do? Did God suffer him to be killed? How did God reward Abraham?

8. Who was Jacob, and where did he live? How many sons had he, and what did they become afterwards? What happened to him? Did Jacob remain in Chanaan? What did he prophesy before his death?

Saviour of the world" (Gen. xli. 45). At his invitation his father, Jacob, and all his family went into Egypt and settled there. Before his death Jacob (1689 B.C.) prophesied, *"the sceptre* (supreme power) *shall not be taken away from* (the tribe of) *Juda* (one of Jacob's sons) *till He come that is to be sent; and He shall be the expectation of nations"* (Gen. xlix. 10).

FROM MOSES TO CHRIST.

9. After Joseph's death the Israelites grew so strong and numerous that the Egyptians, becoming afraid of them, oppressed them and condemned them to very severe labor. But one day the Lord spoke to Moses from the flame of a burning bush, and directed him to lead the Israelites back again to Chanaan. The King, or Pharao, of Egypt refusing to let them go, Almighty God sent dreadful plagues upon the land, and at last an angel of the Lord in one night slew all the first-born of the Egyptians. But the angel spared the Israelites, who had sprinkled the doors of their houses with the blood of the paschal lamb which they had eaten that night according to God's command.

10. Pharao then permitted the Israelites to depart; but he soon regretted it and set out in pursuit of them to the Red Sea. Here Moses, by God's command, stretched forth his rod and the waters opened before the Israelites, who passed over on dry ground. Pharao and his army rushed in after them; but Moses again stretching forth his rod, the waters returned to their place and the Egyptians were buried in the deep (1491 B.C.)

---

9. What happened to the children of Israel in Egypt ? Whom did God appoint to deliver them ? How did He appear to Moses ? Did Moses meet with any opposition ? What did God do to the Egyptians ? Did the angel hurt also the Israelites ? Why did he not hurt them ?

10. Did Pharao continue keeping the Israelites in bondage ? What did he do soon after ? What did the Israelites do ? How were they delivered ?

11. After travelling fifty days through the wilderness the Israelites came to Mount Sinai, where God, amid thunder and lightning, gave them the Ten Commandments, written on two tablets of stone. He renewed the covenant He had made with their fathers, and gave them useful and wholesome laws. But they soon forgot the Commandments and the blessings of God, and they continually murmured. They even made themselves a golden calf and adored it as a god.

12. In punishment of these and other sins the Israelites were condemned to remain forty years in the desert until another and better generation should grow up. Yet God was always good to them, feeding them with bread from heaven, called *manna*, and giving them water from a rock. At length, after Moses' death, they came to Chanaan, or Palestine, the promised land, which they conquered and divided among the twelve tribes (1351 B.C.)

13. The Israelites dwelt happily in Palestine until, contrary to God's command, they began to marry with the Gentiles, or pagans, and thereby fell into the sin of idolatry. But whenever they repented and left their evil-doing God blessed them, and He raised up pious heroes called *Judges*, such as Gedeon, Jephte, and Samson, who rescued them from their enemies.

14. For more than four hundred years the people of Israel were ruled by the high-priests and judges, but they began to desire a king like the other na-

---

11. Did the Israelites now go on straight to Chanaan? How long were they journeying from Egypt to Mount Sinai? What happened at Mount Sinai? Did God give them the Ten Commandments only? What return did they make for all these benefits?

12. How was their ingratitude punished? Did God abandon them altogether? What favors did He still show them? When, and how, did they get possession of Chanaan?

13. How long did the Israelites remain happy in the promised land? What happened to them when they offended God? How did God help them when they repented?

14. Who were the first rulers of the people of Israel? How long

tions. God then appointed Saul for their king (1095 B.C.), and Saul was anointed by the Prophet Samuel. But Saul disobeyed God, and he was succeeded by David (1055 B.C.), who, when only a youth, had slain the giant Goliath. David extended his kingdom and served God. He composed those beautiful sacred songs called the *Psalms*, in which, by divine inspiration, he prophesied of the Redeemer, who was to be born of his family. Christ is therefore also called the Son of David.

15. David's son and successor, Solomon, was a wise and great king, and built a magnificent temple to the Lord in Jerusalem (about 1000 B.C.) In the Sanctuary, or Holy of Holies, of the temple were kept the ark of the covenant, containing the two tablets of the law which God had given to Moses. The people of Israel had no other temple than that of Jerusalem, nor was it permitted to offer sacrifice in any other. But Solomon fell away from the service of God. He married pagan wives and gave himself up to idolatry.

16. After Solomon's death the tribes of Juda and Benjamin formed the kingdom of Juda, of which Jerusalem was the chief city, while the other ten tribes made Samaria the capital of their kingdom, which henceforth was called the kingdom of Israel. The people of this last built a temple for themselves at Samaria and fell into idolatry. But God abandoned them to the pagan king Salmanasar, who destroyed their kingdom and led them away into captivity (718 B.C.) The kingdom of Juda also was punished for its transgressions. Nabuchodonosor

---

were they governed by them? Who was the first King of Israel? Why was he rejected by God? By whom was he succeeded? What can you tell me of David? Was he also pious? Why are his Psalms so very remarkable? Why is Christ also called the Son of David?

15. Who was Solomon? What famous building did he erect? What was kept in the Sanctuary? What did the Ark of the Covenant contain? Had the people of Israel any other temples, or altars? Did Solomon remain wise and good? What made him leave the service of God?

16. What happened after Solomon's death? Which tribes formed

(Nebuchadnezzar) II. took Jerusalem and destroyed the temple and the city (588 B.C.), carrying off the king, Sedecias, and the people into the Babylonian captivity. But the kingdom of Juda was not destroyed for ever, like the kingdom of Israel, that had forsaken the true religion.

17. Juda had been often warned by prophets who spoke the words of God, and who promised pardon to all who should repent. These prophets foretold also, many centuries before the time, the birth, life, teachings, sufferings, death, resurrection, and ascension of Christ, the descent of the Holy Ghost, the destruction of Jerusalem, and the conversion of the Gentiles. The most remarkable of the prophets were Elias, Eliseus, Isaias, Jeremias, Ezechiel, and Daniel.

18. The captivity had lasted seventy years when Cyrus, King of Persia, took Babylon, and by divine inspiration permitted the Jews to return to their country and rebuild the temple at Jerusalem (536 B.C.) When the old men complained that the new temple was not so beautiful as the former one had been, the Prophet Aggeus foretold that the glory of the latter house should be the greater, for the "Desired of all nations," the Messias, should enter it. (Agg. ii. 8–10).

19. Esdras and Nehemias now re-established the divine service and collected the *Sacred Scriptures*.

---

the kingdom of Juda ? Which was its capital ? How many tribes constituted the kingdom of Israel ? Which was the capital of the kingdom of Israel ? Did it remain faithful to God ? How did God punish it ? Did the kingdom of Juda also sin against the Lord ? Was it also chastised, and how ? Was not its punishment less severe than that of the kingdom of Israel, and why ?

17. Did the judgments of God come upon them quite unexpectedly ? How did God forewarn the people ? Did the prophets announce God's judgments only ? What have they foretold of the Messias ? Which are the most remarkable among the prophets ?

18. How long did the Babylonian Captivity last ? How was it brought to an end ? What did the Jews most urgently set about after their return ? Was the new temple as magnificent as the one that had been demolished ? In what was it superior to the first one ?

19. What is to be observed about Esdras and Nehemias ? How did

The people repented sincerely and did not return to idolatry. When afterward Antiochus, King of Syria, commanded the Jews to adore idols, they courageously resisted; many of them, animated by the example of the aged Eleazar and of the Machabees, preferred to suffer death even rather than disobey the law of God (170-143 B.C.)

20. The Jews longed for the coming of the Redeemer who had been foretold, and among the Gentiles also there was a vague expectation of His coming. The Jews still worshipped the one true God, but sects, such as the Pharisees and Sadducees, had sprung up among them, and many honored God by forms and ceremonies only, but were corrupt at heart and evil in their daily life. The rest of the nations, even the enlightened Greeks and Romans, were given up to idolatry and were sunk in the most horrible vices. But as God had promised our first parents, and had foretold through the prophets, He now sent them a Redeemer and Saviour.

HISTORY OF CHRIST.

21. The world was at peace; Augustus Cæsar was Emperor of Rome, and Herod, the Idumean, King of Judea, when the prophecies were fulfilled. Jesus Christ, the Son of God and Redeemer of the world, was born in a stable at Bethlehem in Judea, of Mary, a virgin, descended from the family of David. His birth was made known by angels to the shepherds about Bethlehem, and a star guided the Wise Men of

---

the people then behave? Did they remain faithful to their Lord and God? How did they show their fidelity? Who especially distinguished themselves at that time?

20. What was the prevalent feeling of the Jews and the pagans? How did corruption appear among the Jews? And how amongst the other nations? Did God help mankind, and how?

21. Under what emperor and what king was the Redeemer born? Where, and of whom, was He born? Who was first told of His birth.

the East who had set out to find and adore Him. King Herod was eager to discover the Infant and put Him to death; but, by the Lord's command, Joseph, the foster-father of Jesus, fled with Him and His mother to Egypt, where they remained until Herod's death. Jesus then spent His early life at Nazareth in Galilee, where He was subject to His parents. When He was twelve years old He went up with His parents to Jerusalem for the Passover, and while there astonished the doctors of the law in the temple by His wisdom. At the age of thirty He was baptized in the river Jordan by John the Baptist. As He came out of the water the Holy Ghost descended upon Him in the form of a dove, and a voice from Heaven said: "This is my Beloved Son, in whom I am well pleased" (Matt. iii. 17).

22. About this time Jesus went into the desert, where He prayed and fasted for forty days; then, returning, He began to preach the Gospel—that is to say, the good tidings of God's reign on earth. He proved His divine mission by His holy life, by the truth and beauty of His teachings, and by the miracles He wrought. He chose twelve poor men to be His *Apostles*, or messengers, that they might be witnesses of what He said and did, and might afterwards preach these things to all peoples. The twelve Apostles were: Simon, who was called Peter, and his brother Andrew; James (the elder) and his brother John, who were the sons of Zebedee; Philip and Bartholomew; Thomas and Matthew; James (the Less) and his brother Thaddeus, sometimes called Jude, who were the sons of Alpheus; Simon the

---

and by whom? What did King Herod try to discover, and why? What did St. Joseph do? Where did Jesus spend His childhood after His return from Egypt? How did he live there? What did He do when he was twelve years old? What did He do when He was thirty? What happened at His baptism?

22. What did Jesus do after His baptism? What does the word *Gospel* mean? How did Jesus prove His Divine mission? How many Apostles did He choose? What does the word *Apostle* signify? Why did He choose them? What are their names? How many other dis

Chanaanite, and Judas Iscariot, who afterwards betrayed his Master. He chose seventy-two disciples also, and these, with the Apostles and the others who adhered to Jesus, were the beginning of that society of the faithful which we call the *Church of Christ.*

23 But though Jesus wrought many miracles and relieved much pain and sorrow, He had many enemies, especially among the Scribes and Pharisees, who hated Him for His justice and because He exposed their hypocrisy. At length, when He had restored Lazarus to life and had come up to Jerusalem to eat the pasch in conformity to the Jewish law —for it was then the season—He was received in triumph by the people assembled in the city, and this only increased the rage and jealousy of His enemies.

24. All this Jesus knew. But He sat down with His Apostles to the paschal feast. Taking bread, He gave thanks, blessed and broke it, and gave it to His disciples, saying: *"Take ye and eat; this is my Body which shall be delivered for you."* After that He took the chalice, or cup, with wine in it, again gave thanks, blessed it, and gave it to His disciples, saying: *"Drink ye all of this; this is my Blood of the New Testament, which shall be shed for you and for many unto the remission of sins. As often as you do this, do it for the commemoration of me."* Thus did Jesus institute the adorable sacrament of the Holy Eucharist. Then He promised His Apostles to send them the Holy Ghost, who should teach them all things and abide with them for ever. Afterwards,

---

ciples did he elect, and for what purpose ? Who formed the beginning of the Christian Church ? What did Jesus promise to His Church ?

23. How did the Jews behave towards Jesus ? Why did the Scribes and Pharisees especially hate him ? What special miracle did Jesus perform in the third year of His teaching ? How was Jesus received by the people ? What effect did this reception of Jesus produce on His enemies ?

24. How did Jesus meet His approaching Passion ? How did He celebrate the Last Supper with His Apostles ? What commandment did He give them at it ? What sacrament did He institute by this ?

rising, He went with His Apostles to pray in the garden of Gethsemani, on the Mount of Olives.

25. As He was praying in the garden a band of His enemies approached, guided by Judas, who had gone out from the feast in order to betray Him. Jesus suffered them to bind Him and lead Him before the chief council of the priests, where He was mocked and ill-used. Thence He was led before Pontius Pilate, the Roman governor of Judea, who sent Him to King Herod; but though none of these could find any evil in Him, He was scourged with rods and crowned with thorns. The next day, which was Friday, Pilate, to please the chief priests and the rabble, who preferred the murderer Barabbas to Him, delivered Him up to them to be crucified.

26. Surrounded by a vile mob and loaded with a heavy cross, Jesus was led like a criminal to Mount Calvary, where at noon He was crucified between two thieves. But He prayed for His enemies: "Father, forgive them, for they know not what they do." When He had hung in agony upon the cross for three hours He cried out: "It is consummated; Father, into thy hands I commend my spirit"; and, bowing His head, He gave up the ghost. One of the Roman soldiers who stood near by was overcome with awe, and exclaimed: "Indeed this was the Son of God." Thus Jesus became "the propitiation for our sins; and not for ours only, but also for those of the whole world" (1 John ii. 2).

What did He promise to His Apostles after the Last Supper? Whither did He go afterwards?

25. By whom was Jesus betrayed in the garden? How was He apprehended? Where did they lead Him then? How was He treated before the Chief Council? To whom did the chief priests, and to whom did Pilate, deliver Him up? What did Pilate and Herod think of Him? What else had Christ to suffer?

26. What did they make Jesus carry? Where, and between whom, was He crucified? For whom did He pray while on the cross? How long did He hang on the cross? How did our Lord expire? What benefit did Jesus confer by His death on us and on the whole world?

27. Our Lord's body was taken down and laid in a new sepulchre, and a guard was placed upon it by the Jews. But on the third day, before sunrise, Christ arose from the sepulchre. From His resurrection to His ascension He often appeared to His disciples. He commanded them to preach the Gospel to all nations, and He made Peter the chief pastor of His flock—that is, the Head of His Church—saying to him: "Feed my lambs; feed my sheep" (John xxi. 15, 17). Forty days after His resurrection He ascended to Heaven from the Mount of Olives in the sight of His disciples.

AFTER CHRIST.

FROM THE ASCENSION OF CHRIST TO THE CONVERSION OF CONSTANTINE.

28. Ten days after our Lord's ascension the Apostles, who had in the meantime chosen Matthias to fill the place of the traitor Judas, were assembled for the feast of the Pentecost, when the Holy Ghost descended upon them in the form of fiery tongues, and they began at once to praise God and to preach the Gospel. Great numbers hastened to be baptized and profess their faith in Jesus as the Son of God.

29. The preaching of the Apostles and the miracles they wrought only angered the chief priests, whose hearts were hardened against the truth. They

---

27. What was done with His sacred body? What did His enemies then do? When, and how, did Christ rise to life? What did He do after His resurrection? What did He command His Apostles to do when He appeared the last time among them? How long did He remain on earth after His resurrection? When, where, and how did He ascend into Heaven?

28. Whom did the Apostles choose in the place of Judas? When, and how, did the Holy Ghost come? What change did He produce in them? How was the lame man at the temple-gate healed? What effect had this miracle on the Jews?

29. What effect did the preaching of the Apostles have upon the chief

ill-treated the Apostles and forbade them to preach in the name of Jesus. They even stirred up the evil-minded and the ignorant, so that Stephen, one of the disciples, was stoned to death. Nevertheless the Apostles continued to preach with wonderful success, and among the converts was Saul, afterwards called Paul, who had at first been a zealous enemy and persecutor of the Christians, but who, through the grace of God, became an Apostle of Jesus Christ.

30. The converts in and about Jerusalem served God with great humility, piety, and charity. They were the first Christian community, and with them began the Christian Church. They lived under the law of their country, but in all that concerned religion they were subject to the Apostles.

31. Although many Jews accepted the doctrine of Christ, the greater part of that race remained obstinate. Seventy years after the birth of Christ the Jewish people revolted against the Roman Empire, and a Roman army, in punishment for this, destroyed the city of Jerusalem and the temple, and led into captivity or dispersed the Jews as well as the Christians who still dwelt at Jerusalem. The Apostles began to preach to the Gentile or heathen nations, and with such good effect that within thirty years after the descent of the Holy Ghost there were Christian congregations in all parts of the vast Roman Empire and in many countries not subject to Rome. All these congregations, no matter how far apart, were united in one faith and in one Catholic—that is, uni-

---

priests? What did they do to the Apostles? Who was the first martyr? Did the Apostles, on being persecuted, cease preaching? What can you relate of St. Paul?

30. Of whom was the first Christian community composed? What was their conduct, and how did they serve God? By what authority, and how, did the Apostles govern this first community?

31. Were the Jews all converted? Did those who refused to believe in Christ remain unpunished? What punishment was inflicted on them? With what success did the Apostles preach to the Gentiles? How did the Apostles organize the new Christian communities? Were these communities separated, and independent of one another? Who

versal—Church, under one head, St. Peter. St. Peter, who was the prince or chief of the Apostles, was at first Bishop of Antioch, but afterwards became Bishop of Rome. He suffered martyrdom under the Emperor Nero (67 A.D.), and after this the visible headship of the Church passed to his successors, the Bishops of Rome, who are commonly called Popes.

32. The Christians, whose virtuous lives were a constant reproach to the viciousness of the pagans, were foully calumniated. They were accused of being enemies of the established government, and the priests of the pagan worship, fearful for the downfall of their superstitions, fomented the ill-will. Many thousands of the Christians were thrown into prisons or were exposed to the cruellest tortures, while great numbers of men were put to death. But nothing could tempt or frighten the greater number of them to deny the faith.

33. These persecutions lasted, with occasional intervals, for about three hundred years. Yet during all this time the faith spread, and the very fortitude with which the Christians suffered made many converts among the pagans, so that the blood of the martyrs became the seed of the Church.

34. But at length the Roman Emperor Constantine, while still a pagan, was at war and prayed to God for assistance. At night, it is said, a bright cross appeared to him in the heavens (312 A.D.), and about this cross was the inscription: "In this sign thou shalt conquer." The next day Constantine had

---

was their common Head? What do we call all these communities together? What is the meaning of Catholic? Where was St. Peter bishop, and where did he die? Upon whom did his supremacy over the whole Church devolve?

32. What impression did the spread of Christianity make on the pagans? How did they attempt to exterminate it? Were there many tortured and killed?

33. How long did these persecutions last? Was the Christian religion destroyed by them? What convinced the pagans of the Divine origin of Christianity? With what, then, may the blood of the martyrs justly be compared?

34. Who was Constantine, and what can you relate concerning his

an ensign in imitation of this cross carried in front of his army, and he gained a complete victory over the enemy. From that day he became the protector of Christianity.

FROM THE CONVERSION OF CONSTANTINE TO THE RISE OF PROTESTANTISM.

35. The cross, which had hitherto been the instrument of death for those regarded as the most infamous criminals, became the badge of honor and victory. Rome was the centre of the pagan world and the mistress of nations, and now the temple of Jupiter was turned into a shrine of the Christian faith, and it was crowned with the cross. Beautiful churches were erected everywhere, and Christianity, which had before hidden in secret places, became the religion of the civilized world, while paganism gave way before it.

36. But heresy had already appeared under different forms. Some of the heretics, among whom were the Arians, the Nestorians, the Eutychians, the Pelagians, etc.—called after their founders—gained the favor of princes and industriously spread their false doctrines among the people. Councils were therefore assembled from time to time to settle difficulties among the faithful, to condemn heresy, and to declare the true teaching of the Church. The first council was that which had assembled at Jerusalem under the presidency of St. Peter. A general or œcumenical council is a general assembly of the bishops of the whole world, met together to discuss

---

victory? In what year did Constantine gain the battle and become the protector of Christianity?

35. What had the cross been before this, and what did it become now? Where was it particularly seen, and what did it announce to the world? What became of paganism, and what was established in its place?

36. Were the contests of the Church now at an end? Who were her new enemies? Whence did the sects take their names? How did they behave towards the faithful? How did the Church oppose these heresies? What is the name of a general assembly of the bishops of

questions of faith or morals, and presided over by the Pope or his representatives. Such a council's decisions in matters of faith are infallible.

37. During the early ages of the Church there were many holy and learned men who taught and defended the truths of religion. They are called the *Fathers of the Church*. Among them were St. Athanasius, Patriarch of Alexandria (d. 373 A.D.); St. Basil the Great, Archbishop of Cæsarea (d. 379 A.D.); St. Gregory Nazianzen (d. 389 A.D.) and St. John Chrysostom (d. 407 A.D.), both Patriarchs of Constantinople; St. Ambrose, Archbishop of Milan (d. 397 A.D.); St. Jerome, who made the Latin version of the Holy Scriptures known as "the Vulgate" (d. 420 A.D.); St. Augustine, Bishop of Hippo, in North Africa, one of the greatest lights of the Church (d. 430 A.D.); and the holy Popes, St. Leo the Great (d. 461 A.D.) and St. Gregory the Great (d. 604 A.D). Almost from the beginning of Christianity pious men, eager to devote themselves more completely to a communion with God, separated themselves from the world and led a solitary life as *hermits,* or a life in community as *monks.* The first hermit who is spoken of was St. Paul (d. about 340 A.D.) St. Anthony, who is called "the Patriarch of Monks," is the first who is known to have established a monastery. But the monastic life of Europe is principally indebted to St. Benedict (d. 543 A.D.), who established a monastery at Monte Cassino, in Italy, and wrote a rule for the guidance of his monks; and to St. Columba, or Columbkille (d. 597 A.D.), an Irish monk, who founded at Iona, on the western coast of Scotland, a community which sent out missionaries in all

---

the Catholic Church? When and why are the decisions of a General Council infallible?

37. By whom did God especially illustrate His Church at this time? How are those holy and learned men called? Can you name any of them? Did any other men distinguish themselves in the Church about this time? Who were the hermits? Why did they renounce all comforts? Who were the first and most famous hermits? Who built the

directions. In the course of time the Benedictine rule prevailed over all the other monastic rules in the west of Europe.

38. In the fifth century the barbarians of the north and east of Europe began to invade the Christian nations. These tribes came in great numbers and destroyed almost everything before them. For more than three centuries new tribes were constantly appearing. One of the most savage of the invading hordes were the Huns, whose king, Attila (d. 453 A.D), styled himself "the Scourge of God." In the fear and disorder produced by these invasions learning and the arts of peace were almost entirely neglected, except in Ireland, which for a time was unmolested, and was therefore, after its conversion, able to supply missionaries and teachers for all the north of Europe. Yet through all this dark period holy and zealous men, principally monks either of St. Benedict's or of St. Columba's rule, devoted themselves to the conversion and civilization of the barbarians. Everywhere monasteries sprang up; and as the monks cultivated the soil and offered a refuge to the oppressed or the persecuted, the monasteries in course of time became the centres of thriving villages and towns. The monks, in fact, were in this way the founders of a great many of the cities of Europe. Gradually the barbarians gave up their roving habits and formed settled Christian nations. Prominent among the missionaries of Europe were: St. Patrick (d. 493 A.D), styled " the Apostle of Ireland,'

---

first monastery? Who particularly advanced the Monastic Life in Europe? What rule is generally observed by the monks?

38. What was the cause of the dangers to which the Church was exposed from the fifth century? Which of the barbarian tribes was the most savage and cruel? Who was their king, and what did he call himself? By what means did God subdue the barbarians? How were the monks founders of cities? When was Ireland converted, and by whom? What peculiarity was there in the conversion of the Irish? Who is called the Apostle of the Germans? Where was he born? Of what town was he made Archbishop? What did, then, the monasteries do for the spreading and strengthening of the faith? What emperor in

and St. Boniface, or Winfrid (d. 755 A.D.), "the Apostle of the Germans." St. Patrick (d. 482 A.D.) was sent to Ireland by Pope Celestine, and had the extraordinary grace of converting the entire people, and that without a single martyr. St. Boniface was born in England, and was by Pope Gregory III. created Archbishop of Mayence, and was martyred in Friesland (755 A.D.) To the preaching and teaching of the Church and its missionaries are due the civilization of the barbarians and the permanent establishment of the European nations, and a very great share of the credit for this is due to the monks. The Emperor Charlemagne founded more than twenty-four monasteries.

39. But, unhappily, heresy and schism had separated a large part of the Christians of the East from the Pope, the centre of unity. The Greek or Eastern Church, through the evil influence of the emperors at Constantinople and the ambition or turbulence of some of the patriarchs and bishops, finally seceded from the unity of the Catholic Church (1054 A.D.) This became the cause of political as well as religious misfortune for the East. In the seventh century (622 A.D.) an impostor, called Mohammed, had begun to preach a new religion in Arabia. The religion was a mixture of Jewish and Christian doctrines and observances with pagan superstitions, and it very soon met with great success among the ignorant and semi-barbarous Arabians. The Mohammedans, as these new fanatics were called, made war against the Christian communities of the East, now weakened and corrupted by schism, and after a

---

those days interested himself particularly for the prosperity of the Christian Church, and what did he do?

39. What happened in the East whilst the Christian faith was successfully spread in the West? Who was the chief cause of those disturbances? What was the unfortunate result of all this? Did God suffer all this to remain unpunished? Who was Mohammed? Of what did he form his new religion? How and where did Mohammedanism spread?

while took possession of most of the countries in which this existed.

40. Jerusalem very soon (637 A.D.) fell into the hands of the Saracens, as the Arabians were called. These held it until it was conquered from them in turn by the Seljukian Turks (1079 A.D.), who had become Mohammedans, and were even more cruel than the Saracens. So harshly were the Christian pilgrims to the Holy Land treated by the Turks that upon an account of their sufferings being brought to the Pope, Urban II., by Peter, surnamed the Hermit, the Pope appealed to the Christian people of Europe to interfere. A council of princes and knights was held at Clermont (1095 A.D.), in France, and when the Pope called for volunteers he was answered with the shout of "God wills it!" All who were enrolled for the Holy War put on a badge of red cloth in the form of a cross, and were hence called *Crusaders*, or cross-bearers. The First Crusade was led by the brave Godfrey of Bouillon, who took Jerusalem and was proclaimed king (1099 A.D.) Godfrey refused to wear a crown of gold where his Redeemer had worn a crown of thorns. But before many years the new kingdom was overthrown by Saladin, Sultan of Egypt (1187 A.D.) Still later (1299 A.D.) fresh hordes of Turks, known as Ottomans, gained a foothold in the Greek Empire, and finally took possession of Constantinople itself (1453 A.D.) Thus was

---

40. In what year did Jerusalem fall under the power of the Mohammedans? When was Jerusalem conquered by the Turks? Were they friends of the Christians? What was the cause of the Crusades? Who was Peter the Hermit, and what did he report to Urban II.? What did the Pope do? What did he effect at the Council of Clermont? In what year was the Council of Clermont held? What is the origin of the name of Crusade? What can you relate of the first Crusade? In what year was Jerusalem taken? What can you relate of Godfrey of Bouillon? How long did the Christian kingdom of Jerusalem last? When, and by whom, was it conquered? About what year, and by what Turks, were the Seljukians subdued, and how far did they extend their conquests? In what year, and by whom, was Constantinople taken? Who checked the further progress of the Turks? In what battle, by whom, and in what year were the Turks completely overthrown? What was the result of this victory?

established the Ottoman or Turkish Empire. But the battle of Lepanto (1571 A.D.), where the united armies of the Pope, Spain, and Venice routed the Turks, put a permanent check to any further advance of the Mohammedans against Catholic Europe.

41. Conspicuous in the Crusades had been the military religious orders of knights, among them the Knights Templars and the Knights Hospitallers of St. John of Jerusalem, also known later on as the Knights of Malta. The Knights Templars were finally suppressed by the Church for their irregularities. During this period, besides the orders of chivalry, various religious orders and societies came into existence. Chief among these were the friars, who differed from the monks in not being confined to a cloister. These friars were called mendicants, because they depended for their support upon the charity of the faithful. St. Dominic founded the Dominicans (1217 A.D.), called Preaching Friars also, and Black Friars ; and St. Francis of Assisi founded the Franciscans (1221 A.D.), called Friars Minor also, and sometimes Gray Friars. This last order has several branches—Capuchins, Observantines, Reformed, Conventuals, etc. About the same time the Carmelite monks were changed into friars, and a little later (1256 A.D.) the Augustinian friars were organized. In each of these orders are included orders of women. These orders, by their zeal and learning, helped wonderfully in the civilizing and Christianizing work of the Church. Great schools and universities and charitable institutions arose under the fostering care of the Church, and men of remarkable learning gave an increased development to the sciences, and especially to theology and philosophy, which the monasteries had preserved during the troubled times when

---

41. What military religious orders were distinguished in the Crusades ? What is the difference between monks and friars ? What religious orders came into existence at this period ? What do you say of their influence ? How did the Church encourage learning ? What

the barbarian races were invading Europe or settling gradually down into civilized communities. One of the greatest of these learned and pious men was St. Thomas Aquinas, a Dominican friar, who, on account of his almost superhuman intellect, has been named "the Angel of the Schools" (d. 1274. A.D.) The period from the beginning of the barbarian invasions (about 395 A.D.) to the fall of Constantinople (1453 A.D.) is known as "the Middle Ages."

42. During the Middle Ages numerous and constant efforts were made by emperors, kings, and others in power to interfere with the liberties of the Church. Particularly the Emperor Henry IV. of Germany was accustomed to bestow bishoprics and other religious offices upon unworthy persons, often selling these appointments to whoever would pay the most. But he was sternly resisted by the great Pope St. Gregory VII., and "the right of investiture," as the right of appointing to these religious offices was called, was finally settled in favor of the Church, though not till after many severe trials. New heresies, too, sprang up, such as those of the Albigenses in the south of France, the Waldenses in the north of Italy, the Hussites in Bohemia, and the Wickliffites, or Lollards, in England. An unfortunate schism also broke out, and anti-Popes divided with the lawful Popes the allegiance of the faithful. With all these disorders there were continual wars, which harassed the people and brought about a corruption of morals and a weakening of the faith.

---

learned man of those times can you name? What do we call those times?

42. How was the Church troubled during the Middle Ages? What emperor was a bitter enemy of the Church's work? Who opposed him? How did the Church get out of it? What evil came afterwards in Europe? Which were the most notorious heretics of that time? What fresh trouble added to the confusion caused by the heretics? What was the unfortunate result?

FROM THE RISE OF PROTESTANTISM TO POPE LEO XIII.

43. Martin Luther, an Augustinian friar, and professor in the University of Wittenberg, in Germany, was a man of great abilities but of an unruly disposition. He began to preach (1517 A.D.) against the abuses in the publication of the indulgences granted by Pope Leo X.; but not content with this, he set himself up as a reformer and violently attacked the lawful authority of the Church and the very principles of that authority. Becoming more reckless as he found himself supported by ambitious princes, he rejected many articles of faith. He condemned the holy sacrifice of the Mass and Confession, as well as fasting, prayers for the dead, and other pious practices. He gave leave to monks and nuns to marry, and he broke the vow of chastity he had himself made, and committed the double sacrilege of taking a nun for his wife. His doctrines he declared to be founded on the Bible only. He soon had many followers and imitators. The so-called Reformers shortly quarrelled among themselves, and scarcely any two could be found to agree long in their religious doctrines. John Calvin, at Geneva, taught that "God had predestined a part of mankind, without any fault of theirs, to eternal damnation." The most impious and absurd things were said and done in the name of religion. The fanatics, carried away by their hatred of the Catholic religion, attacked the churches, monasteries, and convents, and demolished crucifixes as well as the pictures and statues in the churches, defiled the tombs of the saints, and destroyed many precious manuscripts and works of art.

---

43. Who was the author of Protestantism? What sort of a man was he? When and how did he begin his conflict with the Church? Did he stop there? What innovations did he introduce? What did he do with regard to monasteries, monks, and nuns? Whence did he pretend to take his doctrine? Did any imitate Luther's example? Did the different sects agree among themselves? Where and what did Calvin teach? How did the heretics seem to understand religion? What destruction did they do?

44. In the hope of peace Charles V., the Emperor of Germany, summoned a second diet or assembly at Spires (1529 A.D.), where it was decreed that until the decision of a General Council Lutheranism should be tolerated wherever it had already spread, and that, on the other hand, the Catholics should not be molested in the practice of their religion. Against this decree the Lutherans *protested*, and thereafter they and all the other sectaries were called *Protestants*. The Protestants appealed to a General Council, which was at last assembled (1545 A.D.) at Trent, in the Tyrol. At this council the new doctrines were examined and condemned, and the many abuses that had crept into the discipline of the Church during several centuries of disorder were vigorously reformed. But the Protestants refused to appear at the council and they defied its decrees. The insurrections and civil wars brought on by the Protestant revolt continued, with scarcely any peace, until the end of the Thirty Years' War (1648 A.D.) Protestantism took different forms in the different countries. In France and Switzerland it appeared as Calvinism. The French Calvinists, who were known as Huguenots, were especially ferocious, and overran most of the southern part of their country, pillaging churches and monasteries, and persecuting all who remained true to the faith. In England the king, Henry VIII., being refused by the Pope permission to put away his lawful wife and take another, declared himself the head of the Church of England, and was zealously assisted by wicked nobles and scheming men who desired to plunder the rich property of the

---

44. In what year, and by whom, was the Diet of Spires assembled? What famous decree was issued there? How did the name of *Protestants* originate? Are only the Lutherans now called Protestants? In what year was the Council of Trent convoked, and what was done by it? Did the Protestants come to it? What was the effect of Protestantism upon Europe? What were the French Protestants called, and what atrocities did they commit? Who introduced Protestantism into England, and for what reason? What is to be said of the success of Protestantism in the south of Europe and in Ireland?

monasteries and churches. In Germany, where the heresy had first broken out, and in the other northern states of Europe, Lutheranism became the prevailing religion. But the heresy, in any form, made little headway in southern Germany, Italy, Spain, Portugal, or Ireland. It was only successful among the mass of the people of England after the cruellest and most wicked system of persecution had been employed for many years. Still, the same, or even a worse, system of persecution was pursued against the Catholics of Ireland for two hundred years without weakening the faith of the people.

45. But God stirred up the zeal of the Catholics, and a glorious era of missionary enterprise began. Learned, heroic, and saintly men dedicated themselves to the diffusion of true religion, and in the face of every danger they brought the consolations of the faith to the numerous Catholics who still remained in the countries won by Protestantism, and they made many converts among those even who had been drawn away by heresy. These missionaries went into far-off lands also. The Jesuits—that is, the members of the Society of Jesus—were particularly zealous in missionary work. Their order had been founded in 1540 by St. Ignatius of Loyola, a man filled with the love of God and a desire to bring all men into the one fold. In India, Japan, and China millions of converts were made, and in the two former countries the glorious apostle St. Francis Xavier was the leader of the missionaries. The Jesuits, Franciscans, and Dominicans strove with a holy emulation for the salvation of souls in America. Canada, as well as the northern and northeastern parts of what is now the United States, were especially the field of the Jesuits and Franciscans, while the Franciscans and

---

45. How was the Church compensated for her loss in Europe? How was this effected? What is said of the Jesuits? What is the name of the Apostle of the Indies? What was the result of his labors? Was Christianity introduced into China also? What can you relate of the work of the missionaries in America?

Dominicans spread out into all the territories conquered in America by Spain and Portugal.

46. Protestantism made no progress after the end of the first century of its existence, but it soon split up into numerous sects which mercilessly condemned one another, though all united in hatred of the true Church. The principal sects were Lutherans, the various varieties of Calvinism (such as Presbyterians, Huguenots, Dutch Reformed, Independents or Congregationalists, etc.), Episcopalians, Baptists, Quakers, Moravians, Methodists, etc. After Protestantism came its natural following, infidelity, which began in England and soon spread into France. The wickedness that prevailed in the French court and among many of the French nobles made the progress of infidelity easy in France. When at last, in 1789, the Revolution took place in France, the infidels were able for a time to suppress the public exercise of the Catholic religion in that country. Churches and religious houses were broken into by a fanatical rabble, and many priests and religious were put to death, while many others had to flee for their lives. But Napoleon Bonaparte, possessing himself of the government of the country, restored the Catholic religion in France and made a concordat, or agreement, with the Pope (1801 A.D.) Still later (1809 A.D.) Pope Pius VII. was carried off a prisoner by the French troops who invaded Rome, but at the defeat of Napoleon, in 1814, the Pope returned to his see. Pius VII.'s successors have been Leo XII., Pius VIII., Gregory XVI., Pius IX., and the present Sovereign Pontiff, Leo XIII., raised to the Papal throne February 20, 1878, the two hundred and sixty-third successor of St. Peter in an uninterrupted line.

---

46. What became of Protestantism ? What was the final result of its alterations and changes ? What was the natural result of Protestantism ? What did the infidels contrive to do ? By whom, and when, was the Catholic Religion restored in France ? How did Napoleon afterward treat Pius VII. ? In what year did Pius VII. return to

47. Although war and disorder almost constantly prevailed throughout the civilized world, learned and holy men and women showed great zeal in defence of the Catholic faith and in works of charity. The enlightening and sanctifying work of the Church became only the more active from the opposition of heresy and infidelity. Among the saints who brought fresh glory to the Church were St. Charles Borromeo at Milan (d. 1584 A.D.), St. Philip Neri at Rome (d. 1595 A.D.), St. Francis of Sales in Switzerland (d. 1622 A.D.), Pope St. Pius V., St. Francis Borgia, St. Vincent of Paul in France (d. 1660 A.D.), St. Aloysius Gonzaga, St. Stanislas Kostka, St. Angela of Merici, St. Jane Frances of Chantal, St. Alphonsus Liguori, and many others. New religious societies were formed as fast as new needs arose. The immense variety of religious bodies sanctioned by the Church are known, according to their mode of life, as monks, friars, regular clerks, congregationalists, brothers, nuns, and sisters. Examples of monks are Benedictines, Trappists or Cistercians, etc.; of friars, Franciscans, Dominicans, Augustinians, and Carmelites; of regular clerks, Jesuits, Lazarists, Redemptorists, Passionists, Priests of the Holy Cross, etc.; of congregationalists, Sulpicians, Paulists, etc.; of brothers, Brothers of the Christian Schools, Brothers of Mary, Xaverian Brothers, etc. Examples of nuns are Benedictines, Franciscans, Dominicans, Ursulines, School-Sisters of Notre Dame (Our Lady), Nuns of the Visitation, of the Presentation, Ladies of the Sacred Heart, etc.; of sisters, Sisters of Charity, of St. Joseph, of Loretto, of Providence, of Mercy, of Mary, of the Holy Cross, of Notre Dame,

---

Rome? Who were his successors? Who is the present Pope? How many Popes have there been from the time of St. Peter?

47. Did the political disorders stop the work of the Church? Name some of the saints who have flourished since the outbreak of Protestantism? How were the changing needs of society met? How are religious divided? Give examples of each sort of religious? What is said of the religious in the United States?

Little Sisters of the Poor, etc. Communities of all these, besides many others, exist in the United States, and they lend a powerful help to the saving of souls.

48. During the eighteenth century infidelity had won a foothold in many parts of Europe, and its effects were soon seen in the disorders that prevailed nearly everywhere after Napoleon's wars. The Church was constantly harassed in its work. The free exercise of the Catholic religion was prohibited by the Russian government of Poland, and in the so-called Catholic countries even of Europe religion often suffered from the attacks of wicked men who had influence in the civil government. Yet the present century has been full of glories for the Church. In England, Ireland, and Scotland, where for more than two hundred and fifty years Catholics had been subjected to great suffering and humiliation, an act was passed (1829 A.D.) which not only made the exercise of the Catholic religion perfectly free, but also restored to Catholics nearly all their civil rights in those countries. In the other parts of Europe Catholicity has been gaining ground, in spite of the bitter opposition of infidels and others, though in a part of Germany and in Switzerland very unjust laws were passed restricting bishops, priests, and religious in their work, and even confiscating the property of the Church. In Asia and Africa Catholic missionaries are as active as ever, and the blood of the martyrs there, as elsewhere, has become the seed of new Christian communities. In the United States particularly, under a free government of the people, our holy religion thrives, and as it becomes better known is daily becoming better liked by non-Catholics. Throughout the civilized world there are indications that Protestantism and infidelity are los-

---

48. What were some of the effects of the infidelity that spread during the eighteenth century? How has the Church recovered herself in England, Ireland, and Scotland, in Germany, in Asia and Africa, in the United States? What of Protestantism?

ing their hold on thoughtful people, and there is every reason to believe that the providence of God is preparing an era of glory for the Catholic Church.

CONCLUDING REMARKS

ON THE HISTORICAL EVIDENCES OF THE TRUTH OF OUR DIVINE RELIGION.

We have now glanced at the history of our holy religion from Adam, our first parent, to our Lord and Saviour Jesus Christ, and from Him, the divine head and founder of our Church, to His present vicegerent, Leo XIII. How sublime and beautiful is the religion we profess! Everything connected with it teaches us that God alone could have given such a religion to mankind.

1. Man has not invented it; God Himself has taught it to us, and has commanded us to observe it. He revealed it by holy men in the Old Testament (¶¶ 6, 11, 17); and in the New, precisely as the prophecies of the Old Testament had foretold. His Only-Begotten, Eternal Son appeared on earth, and confirmed His divine doctrine by numerous miracles, especially by His Resurrection from the dead (¶¶ 21, 22, 23, 26, 27). God has spoken, and no one has a right to be indifferent to His word.

2. The religion to which we belong did not take rise a few centuries ago only; it dates from the beginning of the world. Its first seeds were laid in Paradise when God promised a Redeemer to our first parents after their fall. The whole of the Old Law,

---

What have we now glanced at? What have we chiefly considered in the history of our Religion?

1. Whence does our Religion come? By whom has God revealed it to us? How did Jesus Christ confirm His Divine Doctrine? Is it indifferent which religion we profess?

2. How old is our Religion? How do you explain and prove its great age?

with its sacrifices and wonderful events, was but a figure of the New Law, which contains the fulfilment and accomplishment of the Old (¶¶ 2, 7, 9, 12, and others). The Old Law believed in the Redeemer to come, and the New believes in Him already come. But it is the same belief in the same Redeemer, and therefore it is essentially the same Religion.

3. Although our Holy Religion began with the beginning of mankind, and its history embraces about six thousand years, yet its beginning is not lost in obscure fables of ancient times; on the contrary, its truth is evident to all. For it exhibits, from the remotest antiquity down to the present time, an uninterrupted series, as it were, of universally known facts, which agree with one another, with the monuments of past ages, with the annals of the various nations of the world, and with the discoveries made by natural philosophers. We can name the generations as they succeeded one another from Adam to Christ (Luke iii.; Matt. i.), and all the Supreme Pastors or Popes from St. Peter to our Holy Father, Leo XIII., who is now gloriously governing the Church established by the Son of God. What a wonderful chain!

4. Even the Jews bear witness to its truth. For they keep on record, in their Holy Books, the whole history and all the prophecies of the Old Testament, to which we appeal in order to prove the divine origin of Christianity; so that no one can for a moment suppose that the Christians have perverted or invented such passages in the Old Testament as refer to our Saviour (¶ 17).

5. Nor can it be denied that it is through the help of God that the Christian Religion has spread

---

3. Is the history of our Religion perhaps uncertain, because it dates from the origin of the world and embraces so long a period? Why not?

4. What evidence do even the Jews give to the truth of our Religion? What does this prove?

5. How do you prove that the Christian Religion was spread through

over the whole earth. The apostles who first preached it were poor, unknown, even without eloquence or learning. Their doctrine of the Cross, which contains the mysteries of penance, humility, and mortification, was not likely to please the proud and licentious pagans, who found in their abominable mythology (*i.e.*, fabulous history of their gods) not only an excuse, but even a justification, for all their vices. The rich and the great looked with disdain upon the poor fishermen; the witty and the learned laughed at them; and the mighty rulers of the earth, as even pagan writers testify, took all possible pains to destroy them with fire and sword. During three centuries persecution and martyrdom were the common lot of the Christians. Nevertheless, the doctrine of the poor fishermen, as we have seen, triumphed over all its enemies, and thus proved to be the doctrine of God (¶¶ 29-35). It spread so rapidly that, soon after the death of the apostles, St. Justin ventured to affirm before the whole world, "There is no people, either among the barbarians or among the Greeks or in any other known nation, among whom prayers and thanksgivings are not offered up to the Father and Creator of the universe in the name of Christ Crucified."

6. But not only is the Christian Church founded on miracles; her duration itself is a continual and perpetual miracle. Nations, in spite of their power, perish in the course of time; the dominion of Christ alone outlasts them all, and is constantly increasing. If it decreases in one part of the world it spreads the more in another (¶ 45). From the time of its foundation it has been assailed by enemies from within and without. The Church of Christ has no army to repulse their assaults, no sword to oppose their rude

---

the help of God? About what time did St. Justin live? What does he testify of the spread of Christianity?

6. How do you prove that the duration or permanent continuance of the Christian Church is a miracle?

violence. Had not the arm of God protected her, she would long since have been overcome by her enemies (¶¶ 32, 36, 38, 39, 42, 43, 46, 47).

7. The Christian Church appears still more glorious if we consider the benefits and blessings which she has at all times conferred on mankind. It was she that subdued the brutality of the barbarians, that abolished slavery and human sacrifices, and promoted public and domestic happiness. It was she that founded hospitals and other charitable institutions for the reception of the sick and distressed; it was she that amended laws or made new ones; it was she that taught concord and charity, and diffused learning and true enlightenment (¶¶ 30, 38, 41, 45, 46). We know very well what has become of the nations in Asia and Africa which have lost Christianity, and what harm has been done by infidels in Europe (¶¶ 39, 37, 47). If "the tree is to be known by its fruits" (Matt. vii. 16), every one must see that the Christian faith, which diffuses nothing but happiness and blessings, is the most valuable gift of God; that, on the contrary, infidelity, which produces but misery and vexation, can only proceed from the spirit of evil.

8. Now, this Church which Almighty God has founded on miracles, nay, which is herself a continual miracle; this Church which incessantly pours out the greatest benefits over the universe, can be no other than the Roman Catholic Church. History clearly proves that she, and no other, is that community of the faithful which Christ has established for the salvation of the world, in which the bishops, as the successors of the apostles, under the supreme authority of the Pope, the successor of St. Peter, exercise their teaching and pastoral of-

---

7. What fruits did the Christian Faith produce for mankind? What, on the contrary, were the fruits which heresy and infidelity brought forth? What conclusion must we draw from these different fruits?

8. How do you prove from history that the Church established by God can be no other than the Roman Catholic? What has Christ

fices in an uninterrupted succession (¶¶ 22, 30, 31). It is impossible that any sect, whatever may be its name, should be the Church founded by Christ; for it is well known that every one of them began to exist long after Christ, and that all the sects owe their origin to their separation from the Church of Christ (¶¶ 36, 42, 43). We see, therefore, that in all these sects the words of Jesus are sooner or later fulfilled : "Every plant which my Heavenly Father hath not planted shall be rooted up" (Matt. xv. 13). Their existence is not lasting; they spring up, make some noise, and disappear again. It is not so with the Catholic Church. Thousands of years pass away; she does not vanish, nor does she grow old; for to her our Lord made the promise: "Upon this rock I will build my Church, and the gates of hell shall not prevail against her" (Matt. xvi. 18).

---

foretold of all Sects? What promise has He given to the Catholic Church?

INTRODUCTION.

ON THE END OF MAN.

1. By whom were we created?
We were created by God the Sovereign Lord?
2. Why were we created?
We were created that we might know God, love Him, and serve Him, and thereby attain Heaven.
3. What is meant by 'serving God'?
By 'serving God' is meant doing His holy will.
4. Are we bound to serve God and to love Him?
Yes; because he is our Creator and Sovereign Lord, and the highest and best good.
5. What is Heaven?
Heaven is a place of eternal and perfect happiness.
6. Shall all enter into this perfect happiness?
No; only those that know God, love Him with all their hearts, and serve Him faithfully.
7. What shall become of those who will not know, love, and serve God?
God will cast them from Him for ever.
8. For what end were the things of this world given to us?
That we might use them for the purpose of knowing and serving God.

9. Can the things of this world make us truly happy?

No; they cannot make us truly happy.

10. Why not?

1. Because the things of this world are vain and perishable; and 2. Because man is made for God and for everlasting happiness in Heaven.

11. What, then, is most necessary in this life?

In this life it is most necessary that we should know, love, and serve God, and thereby obtain eternal happiness.

12. What must we do to attain this end?

1. We must believe all that God has revealed; 2. We must keep all the commandments which God has ordered to be kept; and 3. We must use the means of grace which God has ordained for our salvation.

13. Where can we get a right knowledge of these things?

In the Catechism, which contains the Christian Doctrine in question and answer.

14. What, then, does the Catechism treat of?

It treats: 1. of FAITH; 2. of the COMMANDMENTS; and 3. of the MEANS OF GRACE, namely, the Sacraments and Prayer.

PART I.

ON FAITH.

Questions with this mark * can be omitted, at the option of the teacher on first going through this Catechism.

§ 1. *Meaning, Object, and Rule of Faith.*

1. What is Faith?

Faith is a virtue infused by God into our souls, by which we believe without doubting all those things which God has revealed and proposes by His Church for our belief.

2. Why must we believe all that God has revealed?

Because God is the eternal and infallible truth.

3. What means 'all that God has revealed'?

It means all that God has made known for our salvation by the Patriarchs and Prophets, and last of all by His Son Jesus Christ and the Apostles.

*4. How has divine revelation come down to us?

Divine revelation has come down to us partly by *writing*—that is, by the Holy Scripture, or the Bible; partly by *word of mouth*—that is, by tradition.

*5. What is the Holy Scripture?

The Holy Scripture is a collection of books which were written by the inspiration of the Holy Ghost, and are acknowledged by the Church as the Word of God.

*6. How is the Holy Scripture divided?

The Holy Scripture is divided into the books of the Old and the New Testament, or of the Old and the New Law.

*7. What revelations does the Old Testament contain?

The Old Testament contains the Divine Revelations which were made to man before the coming of Christ.

*8. Of what books does the Old Testament consist?

The Old Testament consists of 1. *Twenty-one historical books;* 2. *Seven moral books;* and 3. *Seventeen prophetical books.*

*9. What revelations does the New Testament contain?

The New Testament contains the Revelations which we have received through Jesus Christ and the Apostles.

*10. Of what books does the New Testament consist?

The New Testament consists of 1. The *four Gospels* according to St. Matthew, St. Mark, St. Luke, and St. John; 2. The *Acts of the Apostles,* by St. Luke; 3. *Fourteen Epistles* of St. Paul and *seven* of other Apostles; 4. The *Apocalypse,* or the Revelation of St. John.

*11. Is it enough to believe only what is contained in the Holy Scripture?

No; we must also believe *Tradition*—i.e., those revealed truths which the Apostles preached, but did not commit to writing.

St. Paul, therefore, exhorts the first Christians saying: 'Therefore, brethren, stand fast: and *hold the traditions* which you have learned, whether *by word* or by our Epistle' (2 Thess. ii. 14).

*12. But why must we believe Tradition, as well as what is contained in the Holy Scripture?

Because Catholic Tradition, as well as what is contained in the Holy Scripture, was revealed by God.

13. What, then, must the Catholic Christian believe in general?

He must believe all that God has revealed and the Catholic Church proposes to his belief, whether it be contained in the Holy Scripture or not.

*14. How do we know that it is only from the Catholic Church that we have the Holy Scripture and Tradition?

1. Because the Catholic Church alone has received the Scripture and Tradition from the Apostles; and 2. Because it is she alone who gives us security for their Divine origin.

*15. And why do we say that through the Catholic Church alone we know the true meaning of the Scripture and of Tradition?

Because the Catholic Church alone is 'the pillar and ground of the truth' (1 Tim. iii. 15).

*16. May no one, then, explain the Scripture and Tradition contrary to the opinion of the Catholic Church?

No; for this would be as if he understood the Scripture and Tradition better than the Holy Ghost, who inspires the Church with the true meaning of them.

§ 2. *Necessity of Faith.*

17. Is faith necessary to salvation?

Faith is absolutely necessary to salvation; for *'without faith it is impossible to please God'* (Heb. xi. 6).

'He that doth not believe is already judged' (John iii. 18).

'He that believeth not shall be condemned' (Mark xvi. 16).

18. Will any faith save us?

No; only the true faith, which Christ our Lord has taught us, will save us (John iii. 36).

*19. Why will only that faith which Christ has taught save us?

Because by that faith alone, and by no other, we are made partakers of Christ, and without Christ there is no salvation (Acts iv. 12).

20. Which Church has the true faith taught by Christ?

The Catholic Church alone has the true faith taught by Christ.

21. Why is it the Catholic Church alone that has the true faith taught by Christ?

Because the Catholic Church alone has received from Christ Himself, through His Apostles, this faith as a heavenly gift entrusted to her, and has always preserved it uncorrupted (1 Tim. vi. 20).

Application: Rejoice and often thank God that you are a child of the Catholic Church; for '*there is,*' as St. Augustine says, '*no greater wealth, no greater treasure, than the Catholic faith,*' provided we live as our faith teaches us. The truth of this is especially felt by Catholics at the hour of death.

§ 3. *Qualities of Faith.*

*22. What must be the qualities of our faith?

Our faith must be, 1. *Universal;* 2. *Firm;* 3. *Lively;* and 4. *Constant.*

*23. When is our faith *universal?*

Our faith is universal when we believe not only *some* but *all* the truths which the Catholic Church proposes to our belief.

*24. When is our faith *firm?*

Our faith is firm when we believe without the least doubt.

Examples: Abraham, rewarded for his firm faith: 'In the promise of God he staggered not by distrust, but was strengthened in faith; and therefore it was reputed to him unto justice' (Rom. iv. 20, 22). Moses and Aaron, punished on account of a doubt (Numbers xx. 12).

*25. When is our faith *lively?*
Our faith is lively when we live up to it—that is, when we avoid evil, and do good in the manner which our faith directs (James ii. 26).

*26. When is our faith *constant?*
Our faith is constant when we are ready to lose all, even our life, rather than fall away from it.

*27. What leads people to fall away from their faith?
1. Pride and subtle reasoning on the mysteries of our religion; 2. Neglect of prayer and of the other religious duties; 3. Reading irreligious books and intercourse with irreligious people.

28. How do we especially show that our faith is firm and constant?
By never denying it, even in appearance, and by candidly professing it on every occasion by word and deed (Matt. x. 32, 33; Rom. x. 10).

29. Is there also a particular sign by which Catholics profess their faith?
Yes; the *Sign of the Cross.*

30. When should we make the sign of the cross?
It is good and holy to make it frequently, as the first Christians did; especially when we rise and when we go to bed, before and after prayers, before every important occupation, and in all temptations and dangers.

31. Why is it wholesome frequently to make the sign of the cross?
Because, by devoutly making the sign of the cross, we arm ourselves against the snares of the devil, and draw down the blessings of Heaven upon us.

Application: Never be ashamed of the Catholic faith or of the sign of the cross; let this be your motto: 'God forbid that I should glory, save in the cross of our Lord Jesus Christ' (Gal. vi. 14). Shun most carefully all intercourse with irreligious and wicked persons, and especially beware of such books as might stagger you in the true faith or lead you astray from the path of virtue.

ON THE APOSTLES' CREED.

32. Where do we learn in a few words the chief things which all should know and believe?

In the twelve articles of the Apostles' Creed.

33. Say the Creed.

'I believe,' etc. (See page 6.)

First Article.

'I believe in God the Father Almighty, Creator of heaven and earth.'

§ 1. *On God.*

34. Who is God?

God is an infinitely perfect Spirit, the Lord of heaven and earth, the Author of all good.

35. Why do we call God a 'Spirit'?

We call God a *Spirit* because He has understanding and free-will, but no body (John iv. 24).

36. Why do we say that God is 'infinitely perfect'?

God is infinitely perfect because, unlike created beings, which are good in a limited degree, He unites in Himself all good perfections without measure or number.

37. What are the principal attributes or perfections of God?

God is eternal and unchangeable, omnipresent, omniscient or all-knowing, all-wise, all-powerful; He is infinitely holy and just; infinitely good, merciful, and long-suffering; infinitely true and faithful.

38. What means 'God is eternal'?

God is eternal means that He exists always, and is without beginning and without end (Ps. lxxxix. 2).

39. What means 'God is unchangeable'?

God is unchangeable means that He remains eternally the same, without any change in Himself or in His decrees (James i. 17).

40. What means 'God is omnipresent'?

God is omnipresent means that He is everywhere—in Heaven, on earth, and in all places (Acts xvii. 27, 28).

41. What means 'God is omniscient'?

God is omniscient means that He knows all things perfectly and from all eternity; He knows all things past, present, and to come, even our most secret thoughts (Eccles. xxiii. 28, 29).

42. What means 'God is all-wise'?

God is all-wise means that He knows how to dispose all things in the best way in order to attain His end (Ps. ciii. 24).

Examples: The child Moses saved; Joseph exalted; Aman disgraced.

43. What means 'God is all-powerful or almighty'?

God is all-powerful means that He can do anything, and has only to will and the thing is done (Luke i. 37).

Examples: The Creation; the wonders in Egypt and in the desert.

44. What means 'God is holy'?

God is holy means that He loves and wills only what is good, and that He hates what is evil (Ps. xliv. 8).

Example: The giving of the Law on Mount Sinai.

45. What means 'God is just'?

God is just means that He rewards and punishes men according to their deserts (Rom. ii. 6, 11).

Examples: The world punished by the Deluge, and Sodom and Gomorrha destroyed by fire from heaven; but Noe and Lot saved.

*46. When will perfect retribution be made?

Perfect retribution will be made only in the other world (Matt. xiii. 30; Luke xvi.); but even in this life there is no true happiness for the wicked (Wisd. v. 7) and no true unhappiness for the just (Wisd. iii. 1).

Examples: Joseph, Tobias, Susanna, Daniel, St. Paul (2 Cor. vii. 4).

47. What means '*God is good*'?

God is good means that out of love He will do good to all creatures, and that He really bestows numberless blessings upon us (Wisd. xi. 25).

*48. Which is the greatest proof of God's love and goodness?

That He delivered His own Son up to death for our salvation (1 John iv. 8, 9).

49. What means '*God is merciful*'?

God is merciful means that He willingly forgives all truly penitent sinners (Ez. xxiii. 11).

Examples: The Ninivites; parable of the prodigal son (Luke xv.)

50. What means '*God is long-suffering*'?

God is long-suffering means that He often waits a long while before punishing the sinner, in order to give him time for repentance.

51. What means '*God is true*'?

God is true means that He reveals only the truth, because he can neither err nor lie (Hebr. vi. 18).

52. What means '*God is faithful*'?

God is faithful means that He surely keeps His promises and executes what He threatens (Deut. vii. 9, 10.)

*53. What ought the truth and faithfulness of God lead us to do?

1. To believe in the Word of God and to trust in His promise; and 2. Always to speak the truth and to keep our promises.

54. Can we see God?

No; we cannot see God with corporeal eyes, because He is a Spirit.

*55. How, then, have we come to know God and His perfections, since we cannot see Him?

God has made Himself known to man in various ways.

*56. How has God particularly made Himself known to man?

1. By means of the visible world, which He has created and always governs (Rom. i. 20). 2. By the voice of conscience (Rom. ii. 15). 3. Especially by means of revelations, which He has given us through the Prophets and finally through His Son (John i. 18).

57. Is there more than one God?

No, there is but one God (Isaias xlvi. 9).

*58. Why do we say 'I believe in God,' instead of 'I believe God'?

Because we must not only believe that there is a God, and that all that He has said is true, but we must also give ourselves up to God with love and confidence.

Application: 'My son, give me thy heart' (Prov. xxiii. 26). Oh! give it to Him, the Eternal, the Infinitely Perfect, Rich, Good, and Faithful God, without delay, for ever and ever. God alone has a right to possess it, and He alone has the power to render it happy through all eternity.

§ 2. *On the Three Divine Persons.*

'I believe in God the Father.'

59. Why do we say, 'I believe in God the Father'?

1. Because God is our invisible Father in Heaven; and 2. Because in God there are more than one Person, the first of whom is called the Father.

60. How many Persons are there in God?

There are three Persons in God: the Father, the Son, and the Holy Ghost.

61. Is each one of the three Persons God?

Yes; the Father is true God, the Son is true God, and the Holy Ghost is true God.

62. Are they not, then, three Gods?

No; the three Persons are but one God.

63. Why are the three Persons but one God?

Because all three Persons have one nature and substance.

64. Is any one of these Persons older or more powerful than the others?

No; all three Persons are from eternity, all three are equally powerful, good, and perfect, because all three are but one God.

*65. Is there, then, no distinction at all between the Father, the Son, and the Holy Ghost?

As to the Persons they are distinct; but as to the substance they are one.

*66. How are the three Divine Persons distinct from one another?

In this: that the Father is begotten of no one and proceeds from no one; the Son is begotten of the Father; and the Holy Ghost proceeds from the Father and the Son.

*67. But if the Son is begotten of the Father, and the Holy Ghost proceeds from both, why, then, is none of the Divine Persons older than the others?

Because the Son is begotten from all eternity, and the Holy Ghost also proceeds from all eternity.

68. What works are especially attributed to each of the three Divine Persons?

1. To the Father is especially attributed the Creation; 2. To the Son the Redemption; and 3. To the Holy Ghost Sanctification; although these works are common to all three Persons.

69. What do we call the mystery of one God in three Persons?

We call it the mystery of the Most Holy Trinity.

*70. Can we comprehend this mystery?

No; it is impossible for our weak intellect, which can understand even created things only in an imperfect way, to comprehend a mystery which is infinitely above all created things.

Application: That the grace of this saving faith may not be withdrawn from you, never forget what thanks you owe to the Most Holy Trinity for the inestimable benefits of your creation, redemption, and sanctification, and what you have solemnly promised to the same Trinity in the holy Sacrament of Baptism. (Feast of the Holy Trinity.)

§ 3. *On the Creation and Government of the World.*

71. Why is God called 'Creator of Heaven and earth'?

Because He created the whole world, the heavens and the earth, and all that is in them.

72. What means 'create'?

To make something out of nothing.

73. How did God create the world?

By His almighty will.

'Thou hast created all things; and for Thy will they were and have been created' (Apoc. iv. 11).

74. Why did God create the world?
1. For His own glory; and 2. For the good of His creatures.

75. What does God do to keep the world which He has created from going back into nothing?
He is ever preserving and governing it.

76. How does God preserve the world?
He causes it to continue in the manner most pleasing to Him and as long as it pleases Him.

77. How does God govern the world?
He takes care of all things, orders all things, and directs all things to the end for which He has created the world.

'God made the little and the great, and He hath equally care of all' (Wisd. vi. 8). 'But the very hairs of your head are all numbered' (Matt. x. 30). 'She [the wisdom of God] reacheth therefore from end to end mightily, and ordereth all things sweetly' (Wisd. viii. 1). *Example:* Deliverance of the Jews through Esther.

78. What do we call the care which God uses in preserving and governing the world?
Divine Providence.

*79. But if God orders and directs everything in the world, why is evil done? Does He will it?
No; God does not will evil, but He permits it, 1. Because He has created man free; and 2. Because He knows how to turn evil into good.

Examples: The history of Joseph in Egypt: 'You thought evil against me; but God turned it into good' (Gen. l. 20). Thus God, the Almighty, turned even the murder of our Saviour by the Jews to the salvation of the world, and the impenitence of the same Jews to the conversion of the heathens. And thus He still avails Himself every day of the designs of the wicked in order to glorify His Church; 'for there is no wisdom, there is no prudence, there is no counsel against the Lord' (Prov. xxi. 30).

*80. And if God provides for everything, why is there so much suffering?

1. In order that the sinner may change his ways; and 2. That the just man may increase in merit, and thus obtain a greater reward in Heaven.

Examples: The brothers of Joseph: 'We deserve to suffer these things, because we have sinned against our brother' (Gen. xlii. 21). Manasses (2 Paral. xxxiii.); Jonas (Jonas ii.) 2. 'Gold and silver are tried in the fire, but acceptable men in the furnace of humiliation' (Ecclus. ii. 5). 'Blessed are ye when they shall revile you, and persecute you, and speak all that is evil against you, untruly, for my sake. Be glad and rejoice, for your reward is very great in Heaven' (Matt. v. 11, 12).

*81. How, then, ought we to receive the sufferings that come upon us?

We ought to receive them as graces of God: 'Whom the Lord loveth He chastiseth' (Hebr. xii. 6); and 'before he be glorified' it (his heart) is humbled (Prov. xviii. 12).

Application: 'Cast all your care upon the Lord, for He hath care of you' (1 Pet. v. 7). 'Behold the birds of the air, for they neither sow, nor do they reap, nor gather into barns, and your Heavenly Father feedeth them. Consider the lilies of the field,' etc. (Matt. vi. 26–33). Take willingly everything that is disagreeable to you as coming from the hand of God: 'As it hath pleased the Lord, so is it done; blessed be the name of the Lord' (Job i. 21); and never be so rash as to complain of the dispensations of God. Whatever may come, 'To them that love God, all things work together unto good' (Rom. viii. 28).

§ 4. *On the Angels.*

82. Has God created nothing but the visible world?

God has created also an invisible world—namely, numberless spirits called Angels (Dan. vii. 10).

83. In what state were the Angels when God created them?

They were all good and happy and endowed with excellent gifts.

84. Did all the Angels remain good and happy?
No; many rebelled against God, and therefore were cast into Hell.

'God spared not the Angels that sinned, but delivered them, drawn down by infernal ropes to the lower hell, unto torments' (2 Pet. ii. 4; comp. Jude vi.)

85. How do the good Angels act towards us?
The good Angels love us, and therefore protect us in soul and body, pray for us, and prompt us to do good.

86. How do we call the Angel who is given to every man for his protection?
His Guardian Angel.

87. What is our duty towards our Guardian Angel?
We ought to venerate him with great devotion, thank him, and willingly follow his promptings.

88. How do the wicked Angels act towards us?
The wicked Angels, through hatred and envy, lay snares for us in order to plunge us into eternal destruction.

'Your adversary the devil, as a roaring lion, goeth about seeking whom he may devour' (1 Pet. v. 8). *Examples:* Eve, Job, Sara, the demoniacs, Judas. See also Luke viii. 12 and Apoc. xii.

89. What must we do in order to render their snares harmless?
We must pray and firmly resist all temptations to evil.

Application: Beware of being like the evil spirits by sinning, or of being even their accomplice in seducing others to sin. Imitate the good Angels; be innocent, docile, pious, devout, and always ready to promote the welfare of your neighbor. Daily venerate your Guardian Angel, and recommend yourself to him in all dangers of soul and body. (Feast of the Holy Guardian Angels.)

§ 5. *On our First Parents and their Fall.*

90. How did God make the first man, Adam?

God formed a body out of the earth, and breathed an immortal soul into it; and the first man was made.

91. How did God make Eve?

Out of a rib of Adam as he lay asleep.

92. How did God distinguish man from all other creatures?

By creating him after His own image (Gen. i. 27).

93. How was the first man the image of God?

He was endowed with natural and supernatural gifts which made him resemble God.

94. In what do the *natural* gifts consist?

Especially in this: that the human soul is an immortal spirit, endowed with understanding and free-will.

95. In what did the *supernatural* gifts consist?

Especially in this: 1. That the first man possessed sanctifying grace, and together with it the sonship of God and the right of inheriting the kingdom of Heaven; 2. That in him the senses did not rebel against reason; and 3. That he was not subject to hardships, suffering, or death.

96. Did our first parents preserve these supernatural gifts?

No; through their sin they lost all these supernatural gifts for themselves and for their descendants, and thereby plunged the whole human race into great misery.

97. How did they commit sin?

They believed the serpent rather than God, and ate of the fruit which they had been forbidden to eat.

98. Into what misery have our first parents plunged the whole human race?

Sin, with its evil consequences, has passed from Adam to all mankind, so that we all come into the world in sin.

'By one man sin entered into this world, and by sin death; and so death passed upon all men, in whom all have sinned' (Rom. v. 12). 'Behold, I was conceived in iniquities; and in sins did my mother conceive me' (Ps. l. 7).

99. What do we call the sin in which we are all born?

We call it *Original Sin;* for although we have not committed it ourselves, we have inherited it from our first parents.

100. Who alone of all mankind has not inherited the sin?

The Blessed Virgin Mary, who by a special grace was preserved free from all stain of sin.

*101. What evil consequences have, with original sin, passed to all men?

1. God's displeasure, as well as their loss of the sonship of God and of the inheritance of Heaven; 2. Ignorance, concupiscence, and proneness to evil; and 3. Hardships, suffering, and death.

102. What would have become of man if God had not shown him mercy?

No one could have received grace and been saved.

103. How did God show mercy to man?

He promised him a Saviour, who should take sin away from him, and regain for him grace and the right to the kingdom of Heaven.

104. To whom did God first promise a Saviour?

To our first parents immediately after their fall.

'I will put enmities between thee (the serpent) and the woman'; . . . 'she shall crush thy head' (Gen. iii. 15).

Application: My child, be a beautiful image of God and

hate sin, which has brought all evil into the world. 'Sin maketh nations miserable' (Prov. xiv. 34).

SECOND ARTICLE.

'And in Jesus Christ, His only Son, our Lord.'

105. What does this Second Article of the Creed teach us?

It teaches us that the Redeemer, whom God promised and sent us, is the only Son of God, Jesus Christ, our Lord.

106. How do we know that Jesus Christ is the promised Redeemer?

We know that Jesus Christ is the promised Redeemer because in Him was fulfilled all that the Prophets had foretold of the Redeemer.

107. What had the Prophets foretold of the Redeemer.

They had especially foretold, 1. The time and the place of His birth; 2. The particulars of His Life, Passion, and Death; and 3. The foundation and perpetual duration of His Church.

108. What means the name *Jesus?*

Jesus means *Saviour* or *Redeemer.*

'Thou shalt call His name *Jesus*; for He shall save His people from their sins' (Matt. i. 21).

109. What means the word *Christ?*

Christ—in Hebrew Messias—means *The Anointed.*

*110. Why is Jesus called the Anointed?

Because in the Old Law the prophets, high-priests, and kings were anointed with oil, and Jesus is our greatest Prophet, Priest, and King.

111. Why is Jesus Christ called the 'only Son of God'?

Because Jesus Christ is by nature and from eternity the only Son of God, and as truly God as the Father.

112. And are we not children of God, too?

Yes, but not by nature, and from all eternity; we are only children adopted through grace.

'As many as received Him, He gave them power to be made the sons of God' (John i. 12).

*113. How do we know that Jesus Christ is the Son of God and true God?

1. From the prophecies; 2. From the testimony of His Heavenly Father; 3. From His own testimony; 4. From the teaching of the Apostles; and 5. From the teaching of the Catholic Church.

*114. What do the Prophets say?

They call the promised Redeemer 'God, God with us, the Most Holy, the Wonderful, the Father of the world to come.'

*115. What is the testimony of His Heavenly Father?

At the Baptism of Christ in the Jordan, and at His Transfiguration on Mount Thabor, a voice from Heaven said: 'This is my Beloved Son, in whom I am well pleased' (Matt. iii. 17 and xvii. 5).

*116. What is the testimony of Christ?

Christ testified, 1. That He is the Son of God, and true God, like His Father; 2. He confirmed His testimony by the holiness of His life and by His miracles and prophecies; and 3. He sealed it with His death.

'I and the Father are one. Believe that the Father is in me, and I in the Father' (John x. 30, 38). 'He that seeth me seeth the Father also' (John xiv. 9). 'All things whatsoever the Father hath are mine' (John xvi. 15). 'What things he [the Father] doth, these the Son also doth in like manner. For as the Father raiseth up the dead, and giveth life, so the Son also giveth life to whom He will; that all men may honor the Son, as they honor the Father' (John v. 19, 21, 23). 'Amen, amen I say to you. before Abraham was made, I am' (John viii. 58, etc.) When Peter said to Jesus: 'Thou art Christ, the Son of the living God' (Matt. xvi. 16), and Thomas said to Him: 'My Lord and my God' (John xx. 28), our Saviour confirmed the faith and the declaration of both the Apostles.

*117. What do the Apostles teach of Jesus Christ?

The Apostles clearly teach: 1. That Christ is true God (Rom. ix. 5); 2. That in Him dwells the fulness of the Godhead (Coll. ii. 9); 3. That all creatures should adore Him (Phil. ii. 10 and Hebr. i. 6).

*118. What is the teaching of the Catholic Church?

The Catholic Church has always taught that Christ is true God, and of one substance with the Father; and this doctrine she has ever defended as the chief doctrine of Christianity.

119. Why is Jesus Christ called 'our Lord'?

Jesus Christ is called, and is, our Lord, 1. Because He is our God; and 2. Because He is our Saviour, and has bought us with His blood.

Application: Often call on the name of Jesus with devotion, especially when in temptation. Often use the ejaculation: 'Praised be Jesus Christ'—'For all eternity, Amen!'

THIRD ARTICLE.

'Who was conceived by the Holy Ghost, born of the Virgin Mary.'

§ 1. *The Incarnation of Jesus Christ.*

120. What does the Third Article of the Creed principally teach us?

It teaches us that the Son of God, through the operation of the Holy Ghost, became man—that is, He took to Himself a body and soul like ours.

'The Word [the Only-begotten of the Father] was made flesh, and dwelt among us' (John i. 14).

121. What do we call this Mystery?

The *Incarnation* of the Son of God.

122. What do we believe concerning Jesus Christ when we believe the Mystery of the Incarnation?

We believe that Jesus Christ is both true God and true man: He is God from eternity, and became man in time.

123. How many natures, then, are there in Jesus Christ?

There are two natures in Jesus Christ, the Divine nature and the human nature.

*124. Are there in Jesus Christ two persons also?

No; Jesus Christ is only one Divine Person, for both natures are inseparably united in the same Divine Person of the Son of God.

125. From whom did the Son of God take His human nature?

From Mary, the purest of virgins; therefore she is called, also, the 'Mother of God.' (Feast of the Annunciation B. V. M.)

126. Had Jesus Christ also a father?

As man Jesus Christ had no father, for Joseph was only His foster-father.

'Jesus being [as it was supposed] the Son of Joseph' (Luke iii. 23).

127. Why did the Son of God become man?

That He might be able to suffer and die for us; for as God He could neither suffer nor die.

128. How long since the Son of God came into the world as man?

Over eighteen hundred years.

129. Where was He born?

In a stable at Bethlehem. (Feast of the Nativity, Christmas.)

130. Who were the first that came to adore Him?

There first came shepherds from the neighborhood, and then came the Wise Men, or the Three Kings from the East.

131. How did the shepherds and the Wise Men learn of the birth of Jesus Christ?

The shepherds learned of the birth of Jesus Christ from an angel, and the Wise Men through a star in the heavens.

Application: Give thanks to God with your whole heart for having taken the form of a servant and become a poor child for the love of you, especially when you hear the Angelus-bell ring in the morning, at noon, and at night. Resolve also to perform all your actions in the manner you know Jesus did His. If you do this, you will be sure to please God, whether you be rich or poor. (Feast of the Nativity of our Lord, or Christmas day.)

§ 2. *The Youth of Jesus Christ.*

132. What occurred on the fortieth day after His birth?

On the fortieth day Jesus was offered in the Temple at Jerusalem. (Feast of the Purification, Candlemas.)

133. Did the Child Jesus remain at Jerusalem or in Palestine?

No; Joseph and Mary fled with Him into Egypt, because King Herod sought His life. (Feast of the Holy Innocents.)

134. Where did Jesus live after His return from Egypt?

He lived at Nazareth, in the house of His parents, until His thirtieth year, and was subject to them.

135. Why did Jesus, the Son of God, choose to be obedient?

In order to show by example that children should be obedient to their parents.

136. What did Jesus do in His twelfth year?

In His twelfth year Jesus went with his parents

to Jerusalem, and remained three days in the Temple.

137. Why did He remain in the Temple?

In order to teach us that we should take delight in prayer and study, and should cheerfully spend much time in the house of God.

Application: Often read the life of Jesus and strive to imitate His example, so that you will grow in grace and wisdom.

§ 3. *The Public Life of Jesus Christ.*

138. Where did Jesus go when He was thirty years old?

As soon as Jesus was thirty years old He went to the river Jordan, where He allowed Himself to be baptized by John, and then went out into the desert, where He fasted for forty days and nights.

139. What did He do when He had left the desert?

He began to teach in public and to collect disciples, from whom He chose twelve for His constant companions and called them *Apostles,* or *messengers.*

140. What did Jesus teach?

He taught everything that we ought to believe, to hope for, and to do in order to win salvation.

*141. How did Jesus make known that His teaching was true and divine?

Jesus made known that His teaching was true and divine, 1. By the holiness of His life; and 2. By miracles and prophecies (John viii. 46 and x. 38).

*142. Can you mention some of His miracles?

He changed water into wine; with five loaves He fed over five thousand people; with a word He stilled the wind and the storm; He healed the sick and He raised the dead to life.

*143. Why do we call such acts miracles?

Because they are beyond the natural power of man, and can only be done by the omnipotence of God (John iii. 2).

*144. Can you mention, also, some of the prophecies of Jesus?

Jesus foretold what was known only to God: 1. His betrayal by Judas and His denial by Peter; 2. His passion and death, His resurrection and ascension; 3. The destruction of Jerusalem; and 4. The spread and duration of His Church.

Application: Hold fast to the teachings of Jesus. 'I am the Way, the Truth, and the Life' (John xiv. 6).

Fourth Article.

'Suffered under Pontius Pilate, was crucified, dead, and buried.'

145. What does the Fourth Article of the Creed teach us?

It teaches us that Jesus Christ suffered for us, died on the cross, and was laid in the tomb.

146. What did Jesus Christ suffer for us?

Throughout His entire life He suffered many things. At last, after a great agony, He was seized in the Garden of Gethsemani, mocked, betrayed, scourged, crowned with thorns, and finally nailed to the cross.

147. Who sentenced Jesus to death?

The Roman governor, Pontius Pilate.

148. Where was Jesus crucified?

On Mount Calvary, near Jerusalem.

*149. What happened at His death?

The sun was darkened, the earth trembled, rocks were rent, graves opened, and the dead appeared to many (Matt. xxvii. 54).

150. Did Jesus suffer death against His will?

No; Jesus suffered death of His own free will.

'He was offered because it was His own will' (Isaias liii. 7).

151. **Why did Jesus wish to suffer so much and to die?**

1. In order to atone for our sins and to regain for us grace and Heaven; 2. To show us His great love for us; and 3. To teach us by His own example how to suffer patiently (Isaias liii. 5; John xv. 13; 1 Peter ii. 21).

152. **For what sins did Jesus render satisfaction?**

For Original Sin and for all the other sins of all men.

*153. **But why will not all men be saved?**

All men will not be saved because all do not do what is necessary on their part for obtaining salvation; that is, all men do not believe, keep the commandments, and make use of the graces which God has given them.

154. **What happened after the death of Jesus?**

After death His side was pierced with a lance, then His body was taken down from the cross and laid in a tomb, and they sealed the tomb and set a guard of soldiers to watch over it.

Application: Think often of the bitter sorrow and death of Jesus Christ, and never forget that out of love for us He underwent all. Live and suffer for Him, and remember that by sin you crucify Him anew in your hearts. (Crucifix, Abstinence, and Friday.)

Fifth Article

'He descended into Hell; the third day He rose again from the dead.'

155. **What means 'He descended into hell'?**

That the soul of Jesus Christ, after His death, descended into Limbo to comfort and set free the souls of the just who had died before (1 Pet. iii. 19).

156. **Why were the souls of the just detained in Limbo?**

Because Heaven was closed through sin, and was to be first reopened by Christ.

157. **What means 'the third day He rose again from the dead'?**

That on the third day He reunited His soul to His body and rose again from the grave. (Feast of Easter.)

158. **How did Christ rise again?**

He came forth glorious and immortal from the tomb, although it was closed with a heavy stone and guarded by soldiers.

159. **Did His Disciples see Him again?**

Yes, they often saw Him, and after His resurrection touched Him, ate with Him, and spoke with Him; and they suffered persecution and death rather than deny or conceal the truth of His resurrection.

*160. **How long did Christ remain on the earth after His resurrection?**

He appeared again and again to His Disciples for forty days after the resurrection.

*161. **What did Christ do during that time?**

He conferred upon His Apostles, and especially upon Peter, various powers, and gave various instructions for the good of His Church.

*162. **What effect ought the doctrine of the resurrection of Christ to produce in us?**

It ought, 1. To strengthen our belief in His Divinity and our hope of our own future resurrection; and 2. To incite us to rise from the death of sin to a new and holy life.

Application: Think of what St. Paul says: 'As Christ is risen from the dead by the glory of the Father, so we also may walk in newness of life' (Rom. vi. 4).

Sixth Article.

"He ascended into Heaven, sitteth at the right hand of God the Father Almighty.'

163. What means 'He ascended into Heaven'?

That Jesus Christ, by His own power, with soul and body, went up into Heaven. (Feast of the Ascension.)

164. Did Christ ascend alone into Heaven?

No; he took with Him into Heaven the souls of the just whom He had freed from Limbo (Eph. iv. 8).

*165. From what place did Christ ascend to Heaven?

From the Mount of Olives, in the sight of His Apostles.

*166. Why did Christ ascend into Heaven?

1. To take possession of His glory; 2. To be our Mediator and Advocate with His Father; and 3. To prepare a dwelling for us.

167. What means 'sitteth at the right hand of God'?

It means that Christ, as man also, partakes of the power and glory of the Divine Majesty.

Application: Often turn your eyes and your heart towards Heaven, and shun no pains to win this great reward.

Seventh Article.

'From thence He shall come to judge the living and the dead.'

168. What does the Seventh Article of the Creed teach us?

That Jesus Christ, at the end of the world, shall come again with great power and glory to judge all men, both the good and the wicked.

169. What do you call this judgment?

The General Judgment, the Last Judgment, or the judgment of the world.

170. How shall we be judged?

We shall be judged according to all our thoughts, words, works, and omissions.

171. How will God make known His justice to all the world?

He will make plain to all the good and the evil that every man has done, even his most secret thoughts, and also the graces which He has given to every one.

'The Lord will bring to light the hidden things of darkness, and will make manifest the counsels of the hearts' (1 Cor. iv. 5).

172. What will the Just Judge say to the good?

Christ will say to the good: 'Come, ye blessed of my Father, possess you the kingdom prepared for you from the foundation of the world.'

173. What will He say to the wicked?

But to the wicked He will say: 'Depart from me, ye cursed, into everlasting fire, which was prepared for the devil and his angels' (Matt. xxv. 41).

174. What shall then happen?

The good shall go to Heaven, but the wicked into Hell (Matt. xxv. 46).

175. Is there any other judgment than the General Judgment?

Yes, there is a particular judgment, at which every man is judged at once after his death (Hebr. ix. 27).

*176. Why will a General Judgment take place besides this particular judgment?

A General Judgment will take place, 1. So that the wisdom and justice of God may be acknowledged by all men; 2. That Jesus Christ may be glorified before the whole world; and 3. That the good may receive the reward and the wicked the punishment which they have deserved (Wisd. v. 1–5).

177. Where does the soul go after the particular judgment?

To Heaven, to Hell, or to Purgatory.

178. What is Purgatory?

Purgatory is a state wherein the soul will be purified by suffering for a time.

179. What souls go to Purgatory?

Such souls as have departed this life in a state of venial sin, and such as have still to suffer the punishment deserved for mortal sins the guilt of which has been forgiven.

180. Will Purgatory last after the General Judgment?

No; after the General Judgment there will be only Heaven and Hell.

Application: Do not think that no one sees the evil you are doing; for nothing escapes the eye of God, 'and all things that are done, God will bring into judgment for every error, whether it be good or evil' (Eccles. xii. 14).

Eighth Article.

'I believe in the Holy Ghost.'

181. By whom is the fruit or grace of the Divine Revelation communicated to us?

By the Holy Ghost.

182. Where is this grace communicated to us?

It is communicated to us in the Catholic Church, to which Christ has, for that very purpose, promised and sent the Holy Ghost.

183. Who is the Holy Ghost?

The Holy Ghost is the Third Person of the Blessed Trinity, true God with the Father and the Son.

184. From whom does the Holy Ghost proceed?
The Holy Ghost proceeds from the Father and the Son as from one source.

185. Where is the Holy Ghost?
As God He is everywhere; but as the Author and Dispenser of grace He is especially present in the Catholic Church and in the souls of the just.

186. When did Christ send down the Holy Ghost upon His Church?
On Whit-Sunday, or Pentecost, the Holy Ghost descended upon the Apostles in the form of tongues of fire.

*187. Why was the Holy Ghost sent upon the Church?
To teach, to sanctify, and to rule the Church unto the end of the world.

188. What graces does the Holy Ghost shed upon souls?
He enlightens, sanctifies, strengthens, and comforts them, wherefore He is called the 'Sanctifier' and the 'Comforter.'

189. How long does the Holy Ghost remain in the soul?
As long as the soul is free from mortal sin.

190. What are especially the gifts of the Holy Ghost?
These seven: 1. Wisdom; 2. Understanding; 3. Counsel; 4. Fortitude; 5. Knowledge; 6. Piety; 7. The Fear of God (Isaias xi. 2).

Application: Shun sin, for by it we lose the Holy Ghost and His gifts. 'Wisdom will not,' etc. (Wisd. i. 4, 5).

Ninth Article.

'The Holy Catholic Church; the Communion of Saints.'

*191. What did the Apostles do after they had received the Holy Ghost on Whit-Sunday?

They went out into the whole world, preaching and baptizing, and they united all those who believed and were baptized.

*192. What arose from this uniting of believers?

There arose in many places communities of Christians, whose rulers were the Apostles.

193. What further did the Apostles do when the communities of Christians increased?

They ordained Bishops and set them as rulers over the new Christian communities, with the commission that they likewise should ordain others.

*194. Were all these communities united with one another?

Yes, they were all united, professed the same faith, partook of the same Sacraments, and formed altogether one great Christian community under one Head, St Peter.

*195. What did they call this great Christian community under one Head?

The *Catholic*—that is, the universal—Church, or, in one word, *the Church*.

196. What is the Church?

The Church is, and has always been, the congregation of all the faithful on earth, governed by their lawful Bishops, and united under one visible Head, the Pope.

197. Was the Church thus organized by the Apostles?

The Church was thus organized by Jesus Christ, her Founder; the Apostles were only the instruments of His will.

*198. How did Christ thus organize His Church?

By conferring His own power upon the Apostles and sending them everywhere, 1. To preach; 2. To baptize; and 3. To govern those who were baptized, under the supremacy of St. Peter.

199. Is not Christ Himself the Head of the Church?

Christ is undoubtedly the Head of the Church, but the *invisible Head*.

200. Has Christ given His Church a *visible Head?*

Yes; for as the Church is a visible body, so also must it have a visible Head.

201. How do we know that Christ appointed St. Peter to be the visible Head of His Church?

1. Christ built His Church upon St. Peter, as upon the true foundation-stone; 2. Christ gave to him in particular the keys of the kingdom of Heaven—that is, the Church; and 3. Christ commissioned him alone to feed His whole flock.

*202. Was the Headship of the Church to cease after the death of St. Peter?

No; for as the Church was to last for ever, so also must the Rock upon which He had built it last for ever.

203. Who has been the visible Head of the Church since the death of St. Peter?

The Holy Fathers the Popes, who have been the lawful successors of St. Peter in the Episcopal See of Rome.

204. Who are the successors of the other Apostles?

The Bishops of the Catholic Church, who administer their bishoprics in communion with the Supreme Head, the Pope.

*205. Who are the assistants of the Bishops?

The Priests subject to them.

*206. Who gave the Church this arrangement?

Jesus Christ, its Divine Founder.

*207. How are unity and good order maintained throughout the whole Church?

They are maintained by all rendering a willing

obedience; those who are not Priests, to their Priests, Priests to Bishops, and Bishops to the Pope. Therefore St. Clement, the disciple and successor of St. Peter, compares the Church to an army, in which the privates are subordinate to the captains, the captains to the colonels, and these again to the general.

Application: Always cherish in your heart a profound reverence and an humble submission to the Holy Father the Pope, and to the Bishops and Priests united with him.

*§ 2. *The Marks of the Church.*

208. Did Christ establish one Church, or more than one?

Christ established only one Church, as He taught but one Faith (Matt. xvi. 18).

209. By what marks may the true Church of Christ be known?

The true Church of Christ may be known by these four marks: she is 1. *One;* 2. *Holy;* 3. *Catholic;* and 4. *Apostolic.*

210. Which Church has all these four marks?

It is plain that no Church has these four marks except the *Roman Catholic Church;* that is to say, the Church which acknowledges the Pope of Rome as her Head.

211. Why is the Roman Catholic Church evidently *One?*

Because she has always and everywhere, 1. The same Faith; 2. The same Sacrifice and the same Sacraments; and 3. A common Head.

212. Why is the Roman Catholic Church evidently *Holy?*

1. Because her Founder and her doctrine are holy; 2. Because she preserves and dispenses all

the means of sanctification; and 3. Because she has now and always has had Saints.

213. Why is the Roman Church evidently *Catholic*, or *Universal?*

The Roman Church is *Catholic*, or *Universal*, 1. Because she has always existed from the time of Christ; 2. Because she is to be spread everywhere; and 3. Because she is constantly spreading.

214. Why is the Roman Catholic Church *Apostolic?*

The Roman Catholic Church is Apostolic, 1. Because her origin and her doctrine are from the Apostles; 2. Because the Pope and her Bishops are the rightful successors of the Apostles.

215. If none but the Roman Catholic Church has the marks of the *one* Church of Christ, what follows from this?

That the Roman Catholic Church *alone* is the true Church established by Jesus Christ.

Application: Pray often for the peace and welfare of the Catholic Church and for the conversion of heretics and infidels.

§ 3. *The Qualities of the Church.*

216. Why did Christ establish the Church?

Christ established the Church that by her He might lead all men to salvation.

*217. How has Christ enabled the Church to fulfil her mission?

He has, 1. Entrusted the Church with His doctrine, His means of grace, and His power; and 2. He has sent her the Holy Ghost, so that she might ever preserve the Divine doctrine uncorrupted and rightly dispense the means of grace.

218. By whom is the Divine doctrine always kept pure and uncorrupted in the Church?

By the infallible Teaching Body of the Church.

219. Who compose this infallible Teaching Body?

The Pope, and the Bishops united with him.

*220. Who assures us that the Church cannot err?

Christ Himself in the threefold promise which He made us: 1. That 'He will be with her all days, even to the consummation of the world' (Matt. xviii. 20); 2. That 'the Spirit of Truth will abide with her for ever' (John xiv. 16, 17); 3. That 'the gates of Hell shall not prevail against her' (Matt. xvi. 18).

221. By whom are the decisions of the Church given?

Either by the Supreme Head of the Church, the Pope, giving a decision *ex cathedrâ*, or by a General Council confirmed by the Pope.

*222. Why cannot the Pope teach error when he speaks *ex cathedrâ*?

Because Christ will not allow him to do so; for, 1. Christ made the Pope the foundation of His Church (Matt. xvi. 18); 2. He chose him as the Pastor and Teacher of the whole Church (John xxi. 15–17); 3. He promised him that his faith would not fail, and that he, being confirmed, should confirm his brethren (Luke xxii. 32).

223. What ought we to do when disputes arise in matters of faith?

We must hold to the decisions of the Church.

'And He gave some Apostles, and some Prophets, and other some Evangelists, and other some Pastors and Doctors, for the perfecting of the Saints, for the work of the ministry. . . . Are all Apostles? Are all Prophets? Are all Doctors?' (1 Cor. xii. 18, 29; Eph. iv. 11, 12).

224. What further must we do in order to be saved?

In order to be saved we must be obedient children of the Catholic Church; we must believe her doctrine, use her means of grace, and submit to her authority.

*225. Who teaches us this obligation?

Jesus Christ Himself in these words: ' If he will not hear the Church, let him be to thee as the heathen and publican ' (Matt. xviii. 17).

226. What, therefore, do we profess to believe by these words of the Creed: ' I believe in the Holy Catholic Church ' ?

We profess to believe that Christ has established an infallible Church, which we must believe and obey without reserve if we wish to obtain eternal salvation ; and that this is no other than the Roman Catholic Church.

Application: Honor and love the Church as your mother, and submit humbly to all her decisions, laws, and directions, for ' he shall not have God for his Father who will not have the Church for his Mother ' (St. Cyprian, Bishop and Martyr; d. 258).

*§ 4. *The Growth and Preservation of the Church.*

227. What was the result of the preaching of the Apostles?

A most blessed result, such as only a work of God could have.

228. Why might not this have been the work of man?

Because the Christian Church in an incredibly short time spread over the earth, even while everywhere Jews and Heathen, Emperors and Kings, did their best to check its growth.

229. What did men do to prevent its growth?

Out of hatred for the Christian Church, which condemned their vices, they persecuted the Christians for three hundred years, and put them to death in the cruelest manner.

230. Who gave freedom to the Church at the end of three hundred years?

The Emperor Constantine the Great gave her freedom at last.

231. What led Constantine to do this?

The wonderful appearance of a cross in the heavens with these words upon it: 'In this sign thou shalt conquer'—*In hoc signo vinces.*

232. How long has the Catholic Church lasted?

It has now lasted over eighteen hundred and fifty years.

233. Has the Church had no enemies since the time of Constantine?

The Church has always had many and powerful enemies, but she has not been, and cannot be, overcome.

234. Why cannot the Church be overcome?

The Church cannot be overcome because Jesus Christ has promised that 'the gates of Hell shall not prevail against it.'

235. Who have been the most dangerous enemies of the Church since the time of Constantine?

The most dangerous enemies of the Church have been the heretics who have fallen away from the Catholic Church, and have founded heretical communities or sects.

236. Do these sects last as long as the Church?

No; these sects do not last as long as the Church. They disappear, and others again arise in their place, as the history of each century shows.

237. Did Christ foretell the rise of sects?

Yes; Christ and the Apostles plainly and repeatedly foretold it (Matt. xxiv. 11; 2 Tim. iv. 3; 2 Peter iii. 3; Jude xviii.)

238. Why does God permit sects?

1. Because by their schism from the Church he rids it of its rotten and diseased members; and 2.

Because the doctrine of the Church, through the opposition of these sects, is strengthened and made clearer.

239. How does God supply the place left vacant by the falling away of the sects?

The place of these sects is filled by the conversion of heathen people, who make better use of the grace of Faith.

240. How is the doctrine of the Church strengthened and made clearer?

The teaching authority of the Church, enlightened by the Holy Ghost, declares infallibly what are the ancient Catholic doctrines, confirms them, and condemns the new heresies.

Application: Thank God from the bottom of your heart that you are a child of the Catholic Church, which is so great a blessing. Strive to do honor to your position by leading a good life, for if you do not it will be of little use that you are in the Church.

§ 5. *The Communion of Saints.*

241. Are only the faithful on earth united as one Church?

No; with the faithful on earth are spiritually united the saints in Heaven also, and the souls in Purgatory.

242. In what does this spiritual union consist?

In this: that *all* are members of one body, whose Head is Christ Jesus, and that, therefore, each one shares alike in the spiritual good of the others ('As in one body,' etc., Rom. xii. 4, 5).

243. What is this spiritual union called?

The Communion of Saints.

244. Why are all the members of this communion styled *Saints?*

Because all are *called* to be Saints and have been

sanctified by baptism; and many of them have already arrived at perfect sanctity.

245. What benefit do we enjoy from communion with the Saints in Heaven?

We share in their merits and are helped by their intercession with God for us.

246. What profit do the souls in Purgatory receive from our communion with them?

We assist them by prayer, alms-deeds, and other good works, and especially by the Holy Sacrifice of the Mass and by the application of indulgences.

'It is, therefore, a holy and wholesome thought to pray for the dead, that they may be loosed from sins' (2 Mach. xii. 43, 46).

247. What profit have we from the communion with the faithful on earth?

We share in all the Masses, prayers, and good works of the Catholic Church, and in all her spiritual blessings.

Application: Pray every day for your fellow-Christians who are striving on earth or suffering in Purgatory, and ask every morning and night for the protection of the Saints in Heaven.

Tenth Article.

'The Forgiveness of Sins.'

248. What does the Tenth Article of the Creed teach?

That in the Catholic Church we can receive, through the merits of Jesus Christ, forgiveness of sins and of the punishment due to them.

249. What sins can be forgiven in the Catholic Church?

All sins without exception.

250. What must the sinner do to obtain forgiveness?

1. He must truly repent; and 2. He must worthily receive the Sacraments instituted by Christ for the forgiveness of sins.

251. What Sacraments were instituted by Christ for the forgiveness of sins?

The Sacraments of Baptism and Penance.

252. Who has power to forgive sins in the Sacrament of Penance?

The Bishops of the Catholic Church and the Priests commissioned by them. For it was to them only that Christ said: 'Whose sins you shall forgive, they are forgiven them' (John xx. 23).

Application: Give hearty thanks to God for having promised you forgiveness of your sins, and go willingly and frequently to Confession; but first prepare yourself well for it, that it may be said to you also : 'Be of good heart, son, thy sins are forgiven thee' (Matt. ix. 2).

Eleventh Article.
'The Resurrection of the Body.'

253. What happens to man at death?

The soul leaves the body and appears before the judgment-seat of God; but the body returns into the earth (Eccles. xii. 7).

254. How long will the body remain in the earth?

The body will remain in the earth until the day of judgment, when God will raise it again and reunite it to the soul for ever.

255. What do we call this raising of the body to life?

The resurrection of the body.

*256. Why shall our bodies rise again?

That as the body shared with the soul in good and evil works, so it may also share in the reward or punishment.

257. Shall all men rise from the dead?
Yes, all men, whether good or wicked.

Application: Never abuse your eyes, tongue, ears, hands, or your other senses by doing evil, that you may one day rise to everlasting glory, and not to everlasting perdition.

Twelfth Article.
'And life everlasting. Amen.'

258. What does the Twelfth Article of the Creed teach?
1. That after this life there is another, which shall last for ever; and 2. That the just shall enjoy eternal happiness in it.

*259. Can we conceive this eternal happiness?
No; the happiness of Heaven is so great that we can neither describe nor imagine it.

For 'eye hath not seen, nor ear heard, neither hath it entered into the heart of man what things God hath prepared for them that love Him' (1 Cor. ii. 9).

*260. Will all be equally happy?
No; for 'every one shall receive his own reward according to his own labor'—that is, according to his merits (1 Cor. iii. 8).

261. What will be the life of the wicked for all eternity?
A life without grace or joy, and full of pains, in Hell.

262. Who will be condemned to the torments of Hell?
Every one who dies an enemy to God—that is, who dies in mortal sin.

*263. How do we know that the pains of the damned are eternal?
1. From the plain testimony of Christ and the Apostles (Matt. xxv. 41, 46; Mark ix. 44, 45.

Apoc. xiv. 11, and elsewhere); 2. From the express doctrine of the infallible Church.

*264. Why are the pains of the damned eternal?

1. Because the offence against the infinite Majesty of God requires of His justice an unending punishment; 2. Because all who die in sin remain eternally hardened in sin; and 3. Because only the everlasting pains of Hell are a sufficient means to deter man, even in secret, from evil.

*265. Will all the damned suffer equally?

No; for each shall suffer according to his sins, and according to the bad use he has made of the graces given to him.

266. Will all the damned be damned through their own fault?

Yes; for all men may be eternally happy, if they will use the plentiful graces which God gives them.

'God will have all men to be saved, for there is one mediator of God and men, the Man Christ Jesus, who gave Himself a redemption for all' (1 Tim. ii. 4-6). 'Before man is life and death; that which he shall choose shall be given him' (Ecclus. xv. 18).

*267. What is meant by the *Four Last Things?*
Death, Judgment, Hell, and *Heaven.*

268. What word concludes the Apostles' Creed?

'*Amen,*' which means 'So it is,' or 'So be it.'

269. Why do we conclude the Apostles' Creed with this word?

To declare that we firmly believe all that is contained in the Apostles' Creed, and that we are determined to live and die in this belief.

Application: 'In all thy works remember thy last end, and thou shalt never sin.' Consider that 'once lost, lost for ever.' 'Momentary joy brings on eternal pain, but short pain eternal joy.'

PART II.

THE COMMANDMENTS.

270. To obtain eternal salvation is it enough to believe all that God has revealed?

No; we must also keep His Commandments.

'If thou wilt enter into life, keep my Commandments' (Matt. xix. 17).

271. Can we keep the Commandments of God?

Yes, with the help of God's grace, which He gives to all who ask it.

'His Commandments are not heavy' (1 John v. 3). 'My yoke is sweet, and my burden light' (Matt. xi. 30).

The Chief Commandment.

272. Which is the chief Commandment, that includes all others?

The Commandment of the *Love of God* and of *our Neighbor*. It is also called the *Commandment of Charity*.

273. How is this Commandment expressed?

In these terms:

'Thou shalt love the Lord thy God with thy whole heart, and with thy whole soul, and with thy whole mind, and with thy whole strength. This is the greatest and the first Commandment. And the second is like to this: Thou shalt love thy neighbor as thyself' (Mark xii. 30, 31; Matt. xxii. 37–40).

§ 1. *The Love of God.*

274. What is the love of God?

It is a virtue by which we give ourselves to Him who is the Sovereign Good, with all our heart, in order to please Him by doing His will, and to be united with Him.

*275. What sort of love must we have for God?

1. Our love must be *supernatural;* 2. *We must love Him above all things;* and 3. Our love must be *active.*

*276. When is our love *supernatural?*

Our love is supernatural when, with the help of God's grace, we love Him as we know Him, not only by our reason but by our faith.

'Now the end of the Commandment is charity, from a pure heart, and a good conscience, and an unfeigned faith' (1 Tim. i. 5).

*277. When do we love God above all?

We love God above all when we would rather lose all else than be separated from Him by sin.

'For I am sure that neither death, nor life, nor angels, nor principalities, nor powers, nor things present, nor things to come, nor might, nor height, nor depth, nor any other creature shall be able to separate us from the love of God, which is in Christ Jesus our Lord' (Rom. viii. 38, 39).

*278. When is our love *active?*

Our love is active when we try to please God—that is, when we keep His Commandments.

'He that hath my Commandments,' etc. (John xiv. 21).

*279. Why should we love God?

1. Because He is the sovereign and most perfect Good; 2. Because He has loved us first and has bestowed numberless blessings upon us in soul and body; and 3. Because He commands us to love Him, and promises us eternal salvation as a reward for our love.

*280. When is our love of God *perfect?*

Our love is perfect when we love God above all things, because He is infinitely good in Himself and infinitely good to us.

'Let us therefore love God, because God first hath loved us' (1 John iv. 19).

*281. When is our love *imperfect?*

Our love is imperfect when we love God chiefly because we expect good things from Him.

282. How is the love of God lessened and driven away?

By mortal sin the love of God is driven from our hearts, and by venial sin its fervor is lessened.

Application: In order to exercise yourself in the love of God often think of Him and pray to Him; do and suffer everything for His sake, and fear nothing so much as offending Him.

§ 2. *The Love of our Neighbor.*

283. Whom must we love next after God?

Our neighbor—that is, all men without exception.

*284. Why must we love our neighbor?

1. Because Christ our Lord commands it; 2. Because He has taught it to us by His own example; 3. Because every one is a child and an image of God, was redeemed by the blood of Christ, and is called to eternal salvation.

'Have we not all one Father? Hath not one God created us? Why then doth every one of us despise his brother?' (Mal. ii. 10).

285. What sort of love must we have for our neighbor?

Our love must be, 1. *Sincere;* 2. *Disinterested;* 3. *General.*

286. When is our love *sincere?*

When we love our neighbor really as ourselves (1 John iii. 18).

287. When do we love our neighbor as ourselves?

When we observe the command of Christ: 'All

things whatsoever you would that men should do to you, do you also to them' (Matt. vii. 12).

*288. When is our love *disinterested?*

When we do good to our neighbor for God's sake, and not in order to be praised or rewarded by men (Luke xiv. 14).

*289. When is our love *general?*

When we love every one, whether friend or enemy (Matt. v. 46, 47).

Example: The Good Samaritan.

290. Is it enough if we do not take revenge on our enemies?

No; God commands us to love our enemies—that is, to wish them well, and to be ready to help them in their need as much as we can.

'But I say to you, Love your enemies; do good to them that hate you,' etc. (Matt. v.) *Example:* St. Stephen.

*291. What sort of people does Holy Scripture, in a particular manner, recommend to our love?

The poor, widows and orphans, and in general all who are in bodily or spiritual need.

*292. How are we to help them?

By the Corporal and Spiritual Works of Mercy.

*293. Which are the *Corporal Works of Mercy?*

These seven: 1. To feed the hungry; 2. To give drink to the thirsty; 3. To clothe the naked; 4. To give shelter to the homeless; 5. To visit the imprisoned; 6. To visit the sick; 7. To bury the dead.

*294. Which are the *Spiritual Works of Mercy?*

These seven: 1. To warn sinners; 2. To instruct the ignorant; 3. To counsel the doubting; 4. To comfort the sorrowing; 5. To bear wrongs patiently; 6. To forgive injuries; 7. To pray for the living and the dead.

Application: Be peaceable and kind with every one,

especially with your brothers, sisters, and relations. Never return evil for evil; but pray for those who have offended you.

§ 3. *Christian Self-Love.*

295. May a Christian love himself also?

Yes, he may and ought to love himself; for Christ says: 'Thou shalt love they neighbor as *thyself*.'

296. In what does Christian self-love consist?

Christian self-love consists in being above all things anxious for the salvation of our soul.

*297. What must we be careful to do for the salvation of our soul?

1. We must avoid sin and all occasion of sin; 2. If we have sinned we must do penance at once; 3. We must try to practise virtue and do good works.

298. May we also love our body and the temporal goods of this life in a Christian manner?

Yes, we may and ought, in a Christian manner, to love our body and temporal goods, such as health, property, and our good name.

*299. What is opposite to this *Christian* self-love?

Inordinate self-love.

*300. When is self-love *inordinate?*

1. When we prefer our own honor and will to the honor and will of God; 2. When we are more anxious for our body and temporal things than for our soul and eternal things; 3. When we seek our own welfare to the injury of our neighbor.

Application: Take care to avoid that evil self-love which makes us think, speak, and act only for ourselves, forgetful of the honor of God and the welfare of our neighbor.

THE TEN COMMANDMENTS OF GOD.

301. Where is our duty to God and our neighbor most fully stated?
In the Ten Commandments which God gave to Moses written on two tables of stone.

302. Which are the Ten Commandments?
1. I am the Lord thy God. Thou shalt not have strange gods before me; thou shalt not make to thyself any graven thing to adore it.
2. Thou shalt not take the name of the Lord thy God in vain.
3. Remember that thou keep holy the Sabbath day.
4. Honor thy father and thy mother, that it may be well with thee, and thou mayest live long on the earth.
5. Thou shalt not kill.
6. Thou shalt not commit adultery.
7. Thou shalt not steal.
8. Thou shalt not bear false witness against thy neighbor.
9. Thou shalt not covet thy neighbor's wife.
10. Thou shalt not covet thy neighbor's house, nor his field, nor his servant, nor his handmaid, nor his ox, nor his ass, nor anything that is his.

303. What Commandments were on the first table?
The first three Commandments, of the love and fear of God.

304. What Commandments were on the second table?
The other seven Commandments, of the love of our neighbor.

305. What should lead us to keep the Commandments?
1. The reverence, love, and thankfulness which

we owe to God; 2. The fear of eternal punishment and the hope of eternal reward.

First Commandment of God.

'I am the Lord thy God. Thou shalt not have strange gods before me; thou shalt not make to thyself any graven thing to adore it.'

306. What is commanded by the First Commandment?

To pay to Almighty God due honor and adoration.

307. How many kinds of honor do we owe God?
Two: namely, *inward* and *outward* honor.

308. How do we honor God *inwardly?*
1. By faith, hope, and charity; 2. By adoring Him and thanking Him; 3. By zeal for His honor and by submitting humbly to His will.

309. How do we sin against faith?
1. By infidelity, heresy, and scepticism; 2. By speaking and writing against faith, by reading irreligious books or by listening to them; 3. By indifference in matters of faith, or by actually denying it.

310. How do we sin against hope?
1. By *despair;* and 2. By *presumption.*

311. When do we sin by *despair?*
When we do not hope at all in God, or when we do not hope with confidence in Him.

Example: Cain and Judas; Moses and the Israelites in the desert.

312. What are we to hope for from God?
We must above all hope for everlasting life and whatever is necessary for it—that is, the grace of God and the forgiveness of our sins.

*313. Why must we hope for these things?
Because God, who is all-powerful, merciful, and

truthful, has promised them to us, and because Jesus Christ has merited them for us.

314. What is Christian Hope?
Christian Hope is a virtue from God by which we confidently expect all that He has promised us through the merits of Jesus Christ.

*315. May we hope for temporal goods from God?
Yes, so long as they do not hinder us from eternal salvation.

316. When do we sin by *presumption?*
1. When, relying on the mercy of God, we continue to sin or put off repentance to the hour of death; 2. When we rashly expose ourselves to danger because we think that God will save us from it.

317. How do we sin against the love of God?
By all mortal sins, but especially by indifference, hatred, or distaste for God and his fatherly commands.

318. How do we honor God *outwardly?*
We honor God outwardly when we attend religious services, by kneeling in prayer, and by otherwise showing our respect.

Example: Daniel in the den of lions (Dan. vi.)

319. How do we sin against the outward worship of God?
By neglecting to attend divine service, or by not behaving reverently when we are present.

320. Can we sin in any other way against the honor of God?
Yes, by idolatry, superstition, witchcraft, sacrilege, and simony.

*321. When do we commit *idolatry?*
When we pay divine honor to any creature or thing, as the heathens did.

*322. When do we sin by *superstition?*

1. When we honor God or the Saints in any way contrary to the teaching of the Church; 2. When we impute to things, words, or signs a certain power which they have not by nature, or by the prayers of the Church, or by the command of God.

*323. When are people guilty of *witchcraft?*

When they try, by the help of evil spirits, to find hidden treasures, to injure others, or to work wonderful things.

*324. What is *sacrilege?*

Sacrilege is a profanation of holy things, persons, or places.

Examples: Punishment of King Baltassar (Dan. v.), of Heliodorus (2 Mac. iii.) How Christ cast the sellers out of the Temple (John ii. 15).

*325. When do we commit *simony?*

When we buy or sell spiritual things, preferments, and the like, as Simon the Magician intended to do (Acts viii.)

Application: Every day make Acts of Faith, Hope, and Charity. At church behave with reverence, and pray devoutly on your knees with your hands joined.

First Commandment (*continued*).

The Veneration and Invocation of the Saints.

326. What does the Catholic Church teach as to the veneration and invocation of the Saints?

She teaches that it is right and wholesome to honor and invoke the Saints.

*327. What is the difference between the honor we show to God and that which we show the Saints?

1. We honor God and pray to Him as our Sovereign Lord; but we honor the Saints only as his faithful servants and friends. 2. We honor God for His own sake; but we honor the Saints on ac-

count of the gifts and advantages which they have received from God.

328. What should be our chief object in honoring the Saints?

To become like them by imitating their virtues, in order to share hereafter in their eternal happiness.

329. What is the difference between our prayers to God and those to the Saints?

We pray to God that He may help us by His omnipotence; but we pray to the Saints that they may help us by their intercession with God.

330. Whom should we honor in an especial manner above all the Angels and Saints?

The Blessed Virgin Mary, the Mother of God.

331. Should we honor the images of Jesus Christ and of the Saints?

Yes, certainly; for if we honor the portraits of our parents, we should all the more honor the images of our Lord and of His Saints.

*332. But does not Scripture say: 'You shall not make to yourselves any idol or graven thing'?

Yes; but it adds, 'to adore it,' as the heathen did.

*333. But is it not superstitious to pray before images?

Not at all, as long as we pray not to the images, but to Jesus Christ and to the Saints whom they represent.

*334. Why do we honor the relics of the Saints?

Because their bodies were temples of the Holy Ghost, and will one day rise from the dead to eternal glory.

Application: Honor the Saints, and especially the Blessed Virgin, St. Joseph, and your patron Saint. Diligently read their lives and faithfully follow their example.

Second Commandment of God.

'Thou shalt not take the name of the Lord thy God in vain.'

335. What does the Second Commandment forbid?

It forbids all profanation of the holy name of God.

336. How do we profane the name of God?

1. By uttering it disrespectfully; 2. By blasphemy; 3. By sinful swearing and by cursing; and 4. By breaking oaths or vows.

337. What is blasphemy?

Blasphemy is contemptuous or abusive language uttered against God, the Saints, or holy things.

This sin is so great that, in the Old Law, those who were found guilty of it were put to death. 'He that blasphemeth the name of the Lord, dying let him die; all the multitude shall stone him' (Levit. xxiv. 16).

*338. Can we be guilty of blasphemy in thought?

Yes, when we willingly think with disrespect of God or the Saints.

339. What is swearing?

To swear or to take an oath is to call God to witness that we speak the truth or that we will keep our promise.

340. How do we sin by swearing?

1. When we swear falsely or in doubt; 2. When we swear without necessity, or induce others to do so; 3. When we swear to do evil or to omit what is good; and 4. When we do not keep our oath, although we can keep it.

'Thou shalt swear in truth, and in judgment, and in justice' (Jer. iv. 2).

341. What means swearing falsely or in doubt?

1. To assert with an oath that something is true,

although we know that it is not true, or do not know whether it is true or not; and 2. To promise with an oath what we do not intend to perform.

342. What must we think of perjury or false swearing?

Perjury, especially in a court of justice, is one of the greatest crimes, because he who commits it, 1. Mocks the wisdom and justice of God; 2. Destroys the last means of preserving truth and faith amongst men; and 3. Almost solemnly renounces God and calls down His vengeance upon himself.

'There shall come a curse to the house of him that sweareth falsely in my name, and it shall,' etc. (Zach v. 3, 4).

343. What is cursing?

To curse is to wish evil either to one's self or to another, whereby the name of God is often dishonored.

*344. What is a vow?

A vow is a free promise made to God to do something that is agreeable to Him, although there was no obligation to do it.

*345. Are we bound to keep a vow?

It is a sacred duty to keep a vow, unless it be impossible to do so.

346. Is it enough not to dishonor the name of God?

No; we must honor it by thankfully praising it, piously calling upon it, steadily professing it, and always defending its honor.

Application: Carefully avoid the shameful habit of cursing and swearing. Out of the mouth of a Christian, a child of God, nothing unholy should go forth. 'A man that sweareth much shall be filled with iniquity, and a scourge shall not depart from his house' (Ecclus. xxiii. 12).

Third Commandment of God.

'Remember that thou keep holy the Sabbath day.'

347. What is commanded by the Third Commandment?

To keep holy the Lord's day by doing works of piety and refraining from servile works.

348. Why do we Christians keep Sunday as Sabbath?

Because it was on Sunday that Christ arose from the dead, and it was on Sunday that He sent down the Holy Ghost upon His Church.

349. What pious works should we do on Sunday?

We are bound to hear Mass, and, if possible, we should attend the other services of the Church, especially the Sermon and Catechism. And we should worthily receive the Holy Sacraments.

350. What are servile works?

All bodily works which are commonly performed by servants, day-laborers, and trades-people.

351. Is it never permitted to do servile work on Sunday?

It is, when the pastors of the Church, for weighty reasons, give a dispensation, or in case of urgent need.

*352. Are only those guilty who do such work themselves?

No; all are guilty who, without need, require those under them to do such work, or allow them to do it.

*353. Is Sunday profaned only by servile work, and staying away from Divine Service?

No; it is likewise profaned by debauchery, intemperance, wild sports, and unseemly amusements.

Application: Always observe the Lord's day and do not be led to profane it by excessive fondness for amusement, or by the bad example of infidels, or of wicked men.

Fourth Commandment of God.
'Honor thy Father and thy Mother.'

354. What is commanded by the Fourth Commandment?

It commands children and inferiors to show reverence, love, and obedience to their parents and superiors.

355. Why should children revere, love, and obey their parents?

Because next to God their parents are their greatest benefactors, and supply His place in their regard.

356. When do children sin against the reverence they owe their parents?

1. When they despise their parents; 2. When they speak ill of them; 3. When they treat them harshly or insolently.

'Son, support the old age of thy father, and grieve him not in his life; and if his understanding fail, have patience with him, and despise him not when thou art in thy strength; for the relieving of the father shall not be forgotten' (Ecclus. iii. 14, 15).

357. When do children sin against the love they owe their parents?

1. When they do not pray for their parents; 2. When they grieve them or make them angry; 3. When they do not help them in their need; 4. When they do not bear with their faults.

'He that striketh his father or mother shall be put to death. He that curseth his father or mother shall die the death' (Exod. xxi. 15, 17). *Example:* Jesus even on the cross was watchful for his mother.

358. When do children sin against the obedience they owe their parents?

1. When they obey them badly, or not at all; 2. When they do not willingly take their advice; 3. When they resist their corrections.

'If a man have a stubborn and unruly son, who will not hear the commandments of his father or mother, and, being corrected, slighteth obedience, they shall take him, and bring him to the ancients of the city, and shall say to them: This our son is rebellious and stubborn, he slighteth hearing our admonitions, he giveth himself to revelling, and to debauchery and banquetings: the people of the city shall stone him, and he shall die; that you may take away the evil out of the midst of you, and all Israel hearing it may be afraid' (Deut. xxi. 18-21).

359. What may those children expect who do not fulfil their duty to their parents?

In this life they may expect the curse of God, disgrace, and dishonor; and in the life to come, eternal damnation.

'Cursed be he that honoreth not his father and mother, and all the people shall say: Amen' (Deut. xxvii. 16).

360. What have those children to expect who faithfully obey the Fourth Commandment?

In this life the protection and blessing of God, and in the life to come, eternal salvation.

'Honor thy father and thy mother, which is the first commandment with a promise; that it may be well with thee, and thou mayest be long-lived upon earth' (Eph. vi. 2, 3). *Examples:* Sem, Isaac, and the young Tobias.

361. Whom must we honor, love, and obey besides our parents?

Our guardians, teachers, employers, and all our spiritual and temporal superiors.

362. From whom do temporal and spiritual rulers derive their authority?

From God Himself, who has set them over us for our own good.

'Let every soul be subject to higher powers; for there is no power but from God, and those that are, are ordained of God. Therefore, he that resisteth the power, resisteth the ordinance of God; and they that resist purchase to themselves damnation. Wherefore be subject of necessity, not only for wrath, but also for conscience' sake. Render therefore to all men their dues: tribute to whom tribute is due; custom to whom custom; fear to whom fear; honor to whom honor' (Rom. xiii. 1-7).

*363. How do we sin against temporal and spiritual authority?

1. By impudence and calumny; 2. By disobedience and rebellion.

364. When are parents, or temporal or spiritual authorities, not to be obeyed?

When they ask us to do what is not permitted by God.

'We ought to obey God rather than men' (Acts vii. 29). *Examples:* The three young men at Babylon; the Apostles before the Council.

Application: Honor your parents, teachers, pastors, your lawful rulers, and all whom God has set above you. Obey cheerfully and willingly as did the divine Child Jesus.

FIFTH COMMANDMENT OF GOD.

'Thou shalt not kill.'

365. What is forbidden by the Fifth Commandment?

All sins by which we may injure our neighbor or ourselves, bodily or spiritually.

366. When do we injure our neighbor bodily?

1. When we strike, wound, or kill him; 2. When by annoyance or harsh treatment we embitter and shorten his life.

*367. Is it ever lawful to kill?

Yes; it is lawful, 1. For the supreme authority to do so in the execution of criminals (Rom. xiii. 4); and 2. For others, in defence of their country, or when necessary in protecting life from unjust attack.

368. Does the Fifth Commandment forbid only the taking our neighbor's life?

It forbids also everything which leads to that crime, such as anger, hatred, envy, quarrelling, insulting words, and imprecations.

'Whosoever hateth his brother is a murderer' (1 John iii. 15).

*369. When do we sin against our own life?

1. When we take away our own life; 2. When we impair our health by intemperance in eating and drinking, by violent anger, by immoderate grief, or in other ways.

*370. Should we never expose our life or health to danger?

Never; unless a higher duty requires it (Matt. x. 28).

*371. May we desire our own death?

No; not when the desire comes from dejection or despair, but we may when we ardently desire to be united with God in Heaven.

'I desire to be dissolved, and to be with Christ' (Phil. i. 23).

372. When do we injure our neighbor spiritually?

When we scandalize him—that is, when we intentionally tempt him to sin, or give him occasion to commit it.

373. What should keep us from giving scandal?

1. The thought that he who gives scandal and tempts to sin is a minister of Satan, destroying those souls which Jesus Christ has redeemed with His Blood (John viii. 44); 2. The dreadful consequences of this sin, and the awful sentence of Jesus Christ: 'Woe to that man by whom the scandal cometh' (Matt. xviii. 7).

'He that shall scandalize one of these little ones that believe in me, it were better for him that a millstone should be hanged about his neck, and that he should be drowned in the depth of the sea' (Matt. xviii. 6).

Examples: Eleazar, who chose to die rather than scandalize young men (2 Mac. vi.), and St. Paul (1 Cor. viii. 13).

374. What must we do when we have injured our neighbor as to his body or soul?

We must not only repent and confess our sin, but we must also, as far as we can, repair the evil we have done.

375. What is *commanded* by the Fifth Commandment?

We are commanded to live in peace and union with our neighbor.

Application: Never presume to curse, abuse, or strike any one. Shun a tempter as you would the devil, for he seeks to kill your soul. Beware of killing your neighbor's soul by any scandalous word or deed.

Sixth Commandment of God.

'Thou shalt not commit adultery.'

376. What is forbidden by the Sixth Commandment?

1. Adultery and all sins of impurity, as unchaste looks, words, and jests, and everything immodest; and 2. Everything that leads to impurity (Eph. v. 3, 4).

*377. Why must we carefully guard against impurity?

Because 1. No sin is more shameful, and 2. No other sin is attended with such dreadful consequences.

*378. What are the consequences of impurity?

1. It robs man of his innocence and infects his body and soul; 2. It leads him to many other sins, and often to murder and despair; and 3. It plunges him into misery, dishonor, and shame, and at last into eternal damnation (Ecclus. xix. 3) and (Apoc. xxi. 8).

379. What ought we to do when we are in doubt whether anything is a sin against purity?

We ought to consult our Director, and in the meantime avoid what we are in doubt of.

380. What is *commanded* by the Sixth Commandment?

To be decent and modest in all our thoughts, looks, words, and actions.

*381. What should we do to preserve our purity?

We should, 1. Shun all bad company and all occasions of sin; 2. Often receive the Holy Sacraments; 3. In temptation have recourse to God and to the Blessed Virgin; and 4. Remember that God sees everything and that we may die at any moment.

Application: Think on the words of Holy Scripture: 'Oh! how beautiful is the chaste generation with glory; for the memory thereof is immortal, because it is known both with God and with men' (Wisd. iv. 1). Therefore, whether you are alone or with others, never do or say anything that may not be said or done before decent people.

Seventh Commandment of God.

'Thou shalt not steal.'

382. What does the Seventh Commandment forbid?

To injure our neighbor in his property by robbery or theft, by cheating, usury, or in any other unjust way.

*383. Who are guilty of robbery or theft?

1. All who take away other people's goods, or help to do it, and 2. All who buy stolen property, or do not give up what they have found, or who do not pay their debts.

*384. Who are guilty of cheating?

Those who impose upon their neighbors by false weight or measure, with bad money, or bad articles.

*385. Who are guilty of usury?

Those who ask unlawful interest for the money they lend.

*386. In what other way is the Seventh Commandment broken?

When we damage another's houses, lands, crops, or animals, and, in general, whenever we unjustly injure our neighbor in his property.

387. What must we do when we are in possession of ill-gotten goods or have wrongfully injured our neighbor?

We must restore the ill-gotten goods, and, so far as we can, repair the injury we have done; otherwise we cannot obtain forgiveness from God.

*388. Who is bound to make restitution or reparation?

1. He who wrongfully holds another's goods, or has really done the injury; 2. And if he does not do it, then those are bound to make restitution or reparation who have been accessory to the sin by act or omission.

*389. To whom must restitution of ill-gotten goods be made?

To the owner or to his heirs; but if this be impossible, they must be given to the poor or devoted to other good works.

*390. What must one do who cannot make restitution at once?

He must sincerely desire to do so as soon as possible, and in the meantime he must strive to enable himself to perform this duty.

391. What are we *commanded* by the Seventh Commandment?

We are commanded to give every one what belongs to him, and to be charitable to our neighbor.

Application: Never steal anything, no matter how small, and remember the words: ' A little of one's own is better than much of another's.' Never steal from your parents, for 'He who takes anything from his father or his mother,' etc. (Proverbs xxviii. 24). Brothers and sisters and others of the household are often, through such stealing, unjustly blamed or suspected.

Eighth Commandment of God.

'Thou shalt not bear false witness against thy neighbor.'

392. What does the Eighth Commandment forbid?

The Eighth Commandment forbids above all to give false evidence—that is, to tell a falsehood in a court of justice.

'And bringing two men, sons of the devil, they made them sit against him [Naboth]; and they, like men of the devil, bore witness against him before the people' (3 Kings xxi. 13).

393. What other sins are forbidden by the Eighth Commandment?

1. Lies and hypocrisy; 2. Detraction and calumny or slander; and 3. False suspicion and rash judgment.

394. What is meant by a lie?

To say knowingly and deliberately what is not true with the intention of deceiving.

395. Is it ever lawful to tell a lie?

It is never lawful to tell a lie, either for our own sake or for another's.

'A lie is a foul blot in a man' (Ecclus. xx. 26). 'Lying lips are an abomination to the Lord' (Prov. xii. 22).

Example: Punishment of Ananias and Saphira (Acts v.)

396. How do we sin by hypocrisy?

We sin by hypocrisy by pretending to be better or more pious than we really are, in order to deceive others.

'Woe to you, Scribes and Pharisees, hypocrites! because you are like to whited sepulchres, which outwardly appear to men beautiful, but within are full of dead men's bones, and of all filthiness. So you also outwardly indeed appear to men just, but inwardly you are full of hypocrisy and iniquity' (Matt. xxiii. 27, 28).

397. How do we sin by detraction?
We sin by detraction when we reveal the faults of others without necessity.

398. How do we sin by calumny or slander?
We sin by calumny or slander when we impute to our neighbor faults which he has not at all, or when we exaggerate the faults which he has.

'If a serpent bites in silence, he is nothing better that backbiteth secretly' (Ecclus. x. 11). *Example:* Aman (Esth. xiii.)

399. What ought we to do when we have injured the character of our neighbor by slander?
We ought to take back the slander and repair all the injury we have done.

'A good name is better than great riches' (Prov. xxv. 23).

400. Ought we to retract when we have made known *true* but hidden faults?
In such a case we should try to excuse our neighbor, or to repair his honor by some other lawful means.

401. When do we sin by false suspicion and rash judgment?
We sin, 1. By *false suspicion* when without good reasons we surmise evil of our neighbor; and 2. By *rash judgment* when without good reasons we believe the evil to be true and certain.

'Judge not, that you may not be judged' (Matt. vii. 1, 3).

402. What are we *commanded* by the Eighth Commandment?

We are commanded to be sincere and always to speak nothing but the truth.

Application: Shun lies and falsehoods. Speak kindly of your neighbor; but do not conceal his faults from those who can correct them.

NINTH AND TENTH COMMANDMENTS OF GOD.

'Thou shalt not covet thy neighbor's wife.'
'Thou shalt not covet thy neighbor's goods.'

403. What does the Ninth Commandment forbid?

The Ninth Commandment forbids the desire to have another's wife, and in general all impure thoughts and desires.

404. Are impure thoughts and desires always sins?

They are not sins if they displease us, and we try to drive them from our mind.

405. What are we *commanded* by the Ninth Commandment?

We are commanded to think on such things only as are modest and holy (Phil. iv. 8).

406. What does the Tenth Commandment forbid?

The Tenth Commandment forbids all voluntary desire of our neighbor's goods.

'The desire of money is the root of all evils' (1 Tim. vi. 10).

407. What are we *commanded* by the Tenth Commandment?

We are commanded to be content with our own, and not to envy what belongs to others.

408. Why does God forbid not only evil actions but also evil thoughts and desires?

Because evil thoughts and desires defile the heart, and in the end lead to evil actions.

'Man seeth those things that appear, but the Lord beholdeth the heart' (1 Kings xvi. 7).

Application. Keep your mind free from wicked thoughts and desires, and always remember that the All-wise God knows all that passes through our minds and hearts.

THE SIX COMMANDMENTS OF THE CHURCH.

409. Are there any other Commandments besides those of God which Christians are bound to keep?

Yes, the Commandments of the Church.

410. Whence does the Church get the right to give Commandments?

From Jesus Christ Himself, who charged His Church to guide and govern the faithful in His name.

*411. Can the Church do no more than give Commandments?

She also has a right to see that these Commandments are obeyed, and to punish those who disobey them.

412. Which are the Commandments of the Church?

These six: 1. To rest from servile work and to hear Mass on all Sundays and Holydays of obligation; 2. To fast and to abstain on the days appointed by the Church; 3. To confess our sins at least once a year; 4. To receive *worthily* the Blessed Eucharist at Easter or within the time appointed; 5. To contribute to the support of our pastors; 6. Not to marry persons within the forbidden degrees of kindred or otherwise prohibited by the Church, nor to solemnize marriage at the forbidden times.

413. How do these Commandments of the Church bind us?

They bind us under pain of grievous sin.

'If he will not hear the Church, let him be to thee as the heathen and publican' (Matt. xviii. 17).

Application: Resolve to obey at all times humbly and conscientiously the Commandments and Decrees of the Church, so that one day Jesus Christ may own you as a faithful sheep of his flock, which He has charged St. Peter and his successors to feed.

First Commandment of the Church.

414. What are we commanded by the First Commandment of the Church?

By the First Commandment we are commanded to keep holy the Sundays and the Holydays which the Church has instituted in honor of our Lord and of His Saints.

415. Why were the Feasts of our Lord instituted?

The Feasts of our Lord were instituted so that we might, 1. Meditate on the mysteries of our redemption; 2. Thank God for His graces; and 3. Renew our zeal in his service.

416. Why were the Feasts of the Saints instituted?

The Feasts of the Saints were instituted so that we might, 1. Praise the Lord for the graces which he has bestowed upon them; 2. Resolve to imitate their virtues; and 3. Implore their intercession with God.

417. How are we to keep holy the Sundays and Holydays of obligation?

We are to keep holy the Sundays and Holydays of obligation by resting from servile work and by assisting at the Holy Sacrifice of the Mass with attention, reverence, and devotion.

418. Who are bound to hear Mass on Sundays and Holydays of obligation?

All are bound to hear Mass on Sundays and Holydays of obligation who have come to the age of reason (which is generally about the age of seven), unless excused by weighty reasons.

419. When do we sin against this Commandment of the Church?

We sin against it, 1. When, through our own fault, we lose Mass, or a part of it; and 2. When during Mass we willingly give way to distractions, talk, laugh, or otherwise behave disrespectfully.

'The Lord is in His holy temple; let all the earth keep silence before Him' (Hab. ii. 20).

420. Is it enough if we hear Mass on Sundays and Holydays of obligation?

No; zeal for the honor of God and the salvation of our soul prompts us to attend the other religious services, and especially the sermon and instruction in Christian Doctrine.

Application: Make it a rule to assist with devotion at the Divine Service in the mornings and afternoons on Sundays and Holydays, and to prefer your own parish church to any other.

SECOND COMMANDMENT OF THE CHURCH.

421. What are we commanded by the Second Commandment of the Church?

We are commanded by the Second Commandment to observe the days of fasting and abstinence appointed by the Church.

422. Which are Fast-days?

The Fast-days are:

1. The *Forty Days of Lent*—that is, every day from Ash-Wednesday to Easter, Sundays excepted;
2. The *Ember Days*—that is, Wednesday, Friday,

and Saturday at the beginning of each of the four seasons; 3. The *Vigils* or Eves of certain Feasts; 4. The Fridays of Advent.

In most parts of North America there are five Vigils—viz., Christmas Eve, Easter Eve, Eve of Pentecost or Whit-Saturday, the Eve of the Assumption, and the Eve of All Saints.

*423. Is it sufficient to abstain from flesh-meat on these fast-days?

No; we must also not eat more than one meal, and that not before noon. But a small collation at night is not forbidden.

*424. Who are bound to fast?

All Christians who have completed the age of twenty-one are bound to fast, unless excused by some just cause.

425. When are we commanded to abstain from flesh-meat?

We are commanded to abstain from flesh-meat, unless dispensed, 1. On all Fridays and Saturdays (Christmas-day excepted); 2. On the Sundays of Lent; and 3. On all fast-days.

Our holy mother the Church has judged it expedient to mitigate the severity of this ancient and general law, in modern times, by dispensations which vary somewhat, according to the different conditions of life, in various countries. In virtue of those for the United States, 1. Saturday is not a day of abstinence unless it be also a fast-day; 2. Meat is allowed on all the Sundays of Lent, without restriction as to times; 3. On some other days each week in Lent, to be annually appointed for each diocese by the Bishop, meat is also allowed at the dinner or principal meal. But when meat is so used by dispensation at the principal meal on a fast-day or on a Sunday in Lent, fish cannot be used at the same meal. Every one is bound to conform to the regulations and the practice approved of by the Bishop or ecclesiastical superior of his diocese.

426. Who are bound to abstain from flesh-meat?

All Christians who have reached the age of seven are bound to abstain from flesh-meat, unless excused by some just cause.

*427. What are those to do who cannot well abstain from flesh-meat?

Those who cannot well abstain from flesh-meat must apply to the Bishop, through their Pastor, for a dispensation, and must perform other good works instead.

*428. Why ought we to keep the days of fasting and abstinence?

We ought to keep the days of fasting and abstinence in order, 1. To follow the example of Jesus Christ and of all the Saints; 2. To do penance for our sins; 3. To subdue more easily our wicked desires; and 4. To show our obedience to our holy Mother the Church.

'Be converted unto me with all your heart, in fasting, and in weeping, and in mourning' (Joel ii. 12).

Application: Respect the Commandment of fasting and abstinence as a Commandment which God Himself has given you through His Church, and consider it an honor to observe it strictly.

Third, Fourth, and Fifth Commandments of the Church.

429. What are we commanded by the Third and Fourth Commandments of the Church?

We are commanded by the Third and Fourth Commandments, 1. To confess our sins faithfully at least once a year; and 2. To receive the Holy Communion worthily at Easter or thereabouts.

430. To whom must our confession be made?

To any Priest authorized by the Bishop to hear confessions?

431. Where must we receive Easter Communion?

We must receive Easter Communion in the parish church, if possible, unless we have received permission to do otherwise.

*432. Is it enough if we receive Holy Communion once a year?

No; it is the intention and earnest desire of our holy Mother the Church that we should very often partake of this grace.

Application: Make it a rule to go to Confession and Holy Communion once a month.

433. What are we commanded by the Fifth Commandment of the Church?

We are commanded to contribute willingly according to our means to the support of our Pastors and our churches, and of religious institutions.

St. Paul says: 'So the Lord ordained, that they who preach the Gospel should live by the Gospel' (Cor. ix. 13, 14).

(On the Sixth Commandment of the Church, see the *Sacrament of Matrimony*.)

On the Violation of the Commandments.

§ 1. *On Sin in General.*

434. What is sin?

Sin is a wilful violation of the Law of God.

435. In how many ways may we sin?

We may sin, 1. By *bad* thoughts, desires, words, and actions; and 2. By the omission of the *good* that we are bound to do.

436. Are all sins equally grievous?

No; there are grievous sins which are called *mortal*, and there are lesser ones called *venial*.

Some sins in the Holy Scripture are compared to *motes*, and others to *beams* (Matt. vii. 3).

437. What is mortal sin?

Mortal sin is a wilful violation of the Law of God in an important matter.

438. Why are grievous sins called *mortal*?

They are called *mortal* because they take away the supernatural life of the soul, which is sanctifying grace; and because they bring everlasting death and damnation upon the soul.

'Thou hast the name of being alive and thou art dead' (Apoc. iii. 1).

439. What is *venial* sin?

Venial sin is a transgression of God's Law in a small matter, or a transgression that is not quite wilful.

*440. When is the transgression not quite wilful?

A transgression is not quite wilful when we do not plainly see the evil or do not fully consent to it.

441. Why are lesser sins called *venial*?

They are called *venial* because they can be more easily forgiven, and even without confession.

442. Should we fear only grievous sin?

No, we must fear and detest all sins, whether mortal or venial, as the greatest evil on earth.

'How can I do this wicked thing, and sin against my God' (Gen. xxxix. 9).

443. What should keep us from committing sin?

The consideration of its wickedness and evil consequences.

444. Wherein consists the wickedness of mortal sin?

The wickedness of mortal sin consists in this: 1. It is a grievous offence against God, our Supreme Lord; 2. It is shameful ingratitude to God, our best Father; and 3. It is detestable infidelity to our Redeemer, whom we should love above all things.

445. What best shows the wickedness of sin?

1. The severe punishment of the bad angels and of our first parents; 2. The everlasting punishment in hell which every mortal sin deserves; and 3. The bitter Passion and Death which the Only Son of God had suffered, in order to atone for our sins.

446. What are the consequences of mortal sin?

Mortal sin, 1. Separates us from the friendship and love of God; 2. It robs us of all merits and of our right to Heaven; and 3. It brings upon us the judgment of God, and at last everlasting damnation.

'They that commit sin and iniquity are enemies of their own soul' (Tob. xii. 10). *Examples:* Cain, Judas; Parable of the rich man.

447. Why should we carefully avoid venial sin?

1. Because venial sin also is an offence against God; 2. Because it hinders many graces which God intends to give us; 3. Because it brings many punishments of God upon us; and 4. Because it gradually leads to more serious sins.

'He that is unjust in that which is little is unjust also in that which is greater' (Luke xvi. 10).

Application: 'My son, all the days of thy life have God in thy mind, and take heed thou never consent to sin. . . . We lead indeed a poor life; but we shall have many good things, if we fear God, and depart from all sin, and do that which is good' (Tob. iv. 6, 23).

§ 2. *On the different kinds of Sin.*

448. Which are the principal kinds of sin?

The principal kinds of sin are: 1. The Seven Capital or Deadly Sins; 2. The Six Sins against the Holy Ghost; 3. The Four Sins that cry to Heaven for vengeance; and 4. The nine ways of being accessory to another's sin.

449. Which are the seven *Capital Sins*?

The seven *Capital Sins* are: 1. Pride; 2. Covetousness; 3. Lust; 4. Anger; 5. Gluttony; 6. Envy; and 7. Sloth.

450. Why are they called *Capital* Sins?

They are called Capital Sins because they are the fountain-head or source of all other sins.

451. When do we sin by *Pride?*

We sin by Pride when we think too much of ourselves, do not give due honor to God, and despise our neighbor.

'Pride is hateful before God and men. It is the beginning of all sin. (Ecclus. x. 7, 15). *Examples:* Lucifer, Nabuchodonosor, Holofernes, the Pharisee in the Temple.

452. When do we sin by *Covetousness?*

We sin by Covetousness when we unreasonably seek money and worldly goods, and are hard-hearted to those in distress.

'There is not a more wicked thing than to love money; for such a one setteth even his own soul to sale' (Ecclus. x. 10). *Examples:* Achab, Giezi, Judas.

453. How do we sin by *Lust?*

By indulging in immodest thoughts, desires, words, or actions.

(See the Sixth Commandment of God.)

454. When do we sin by *Anger?*

We sin by Anger when we fly into a passion at what displeases us, and indulge a desire of revenge.

'Let all bitterness, and anger, and indignation, and clamor, and blasphemy be put away from you, with all malice' (Ephes. iv. 31).

Example: Esau, while in anger, designs to kill his brother Jacob.

455. When do we sin by *Gluttony?*

We sin by Gluttony when we eat or drink too much or greedily.

'Their God is their belly' (Philip. iii. 19).

456. When do we sin by *Envy?*

We sin by Envy when we are displeased at the good fortune of our neighbor, or glad of his misfortune.

'By the envy of the devil death came into the world: and they follow him that are of his side' (Wisd. ii. 24, 25).

Examples: Satan, Cain, Joseph's brethren, the Pharisees.

457. **When do we sin by *Sloth*?**

We sin by Sloth when we give way to laziness, and thus neglect our duties.

'Go to the ant, O sluggard, and consider her ways, and learn wisdom' (Prov. vi. 6). With regard to *Spiritual Sloth,* or Lukewarmness in the service of God, our Lord says: 'I would thou wert cold or hot! But because thou art lukewarm, and neither cold nor hot, I will begin to vomit thee out of my mouth' (Apoc. iii. 16).

Examples: The slothful servant; the foolish virgins (Matt. xxv.)

458. **Which are the Six Sins against the Holy Ghost?**

The Six Sins against the Holy Ghost are: 1. Presumption of God's mercy; 2. Despair; 3. Resistance to the known Christian truth; 4. Envy at another's spiritual good; 5. Obstinacy in sin; and 6. Final impenitence.

Examples: Cain, Pharao, the Pharisees, Elymas the magician (Acts. xiii.)

459. **Why are they called sins against the Holy Ghost?**

They are called sins against the Holy Ghost because they are opposed especially to the grace of the Holy Ghost.

*460. **Which are the Four Sins that cry to Heaven for vengeance?**

The Four Sins that cry to Heaven for vengeance are: 1. Wilful murder; 2. Sodomy; 3. Oppression of the poor, and of widows and orphans; 4. Defrauding laborers of their wages.

*461. Why are they said to cry to Heaven for vengeance?

Because on account of their horrible wickedness they seem to cry out to Heaven for punishment.

462. Which are the nine ways of being accessory to another's sin?

The nine ways of being accessory to another's sin are these: 1. By counsel; 2. By command; 3. By consent; 4. By provocation; 5. By praise or flattery; 6. By silence; 7. By connivance; 8. By partaking; 9. By defence of the ill done.

463. When are we answerable for another's sin?

Whenever in any of those nine ways we are the cause of his sin or contribute to it.

Application: Every morning, when you get up, resolve to guard most carefully during the day against your chief fault. At night examine your conscience on it; and if you have failed, repent, and purpose to confess it as soon as possible. Always take good advice thankfully, and be careful not to be accessory to another's sin.

On Virtue and Christian Perfection.

464. Is it enough if we avoid sin and crime?

No; we must also try to become more and more virtuous, and to reach the perfection suitable to our state.

'He that is just, let him be justified still; and he that is holy, let him be sanctified still' (Apoc. xxii. 11).

§ 1. *On Virtue.*

465. Why should we try to become more and more virtuous?

Because the more virtuous we are, the better we are, and the more pleasing to God.

466. In what does Christian virtue consist?

Christian virtue consists in the constant will and effort to do what is pleasing to God.

*467. How many classes of Virtues are there?

There are two classes of Virtues: *Theological* and *Moral* Virtues.

*468. Which are the *Theological Virtues?*

The Theological Virtues are Faith, Hope, and Charity.

*469. Why are these Virtues called Theological?

These virtues are called Theological because they come directly from God and directly relate to Him.

470. When should we make acts of Faith, Hope, and Charity?

We should often make acts of Faith, Hope, and Charity, but especially, 1. When tempted against these virtues; 2. When we receive the Holy Sacraments; and 3. When we are in danger of death.

471. How may we make acts of Faith, Hope, and Charity?

We may make them in the following manner:

AN ACT OF FAITH.

O my God, I firmly believe all the sacred truths which Thy Holy Catholic Church believes and teaches, because Thou hast revealed them, who neither canst deceive nor be deceived.

AN ACT OF HOPE.

O my God, relying on Thy almighty power and Thy infinite mercy and goodness, and because Thou art faithful to Thy promises, I hope to obtain the pardon of my sins, the assistance of Thy grace, and life everlasting, through the merits of Jesus Christ, our Lord and Saviour.

AN ACT OF CHARITY.

O my God, I love Thee above all things with my

whole heart and soul, purely because Thou art infinitely perfect and deserving of all love. I also love my neighbor as myself for the love of Thee. I forgive all who have injured me, and ask pardon of all whom I have injured. Amen.

*472. What do we call those Virtues which can be acquired by practice?

Those virtues which can be acquired by practice we call *Moral Virtues*, because they guide our moral life according to the will of God.

*473. Which are the four *Cardinal Virtues* in which all others are included?

The four Cardinal Virtues are, 1. Prudence; 2. Justice; 3. Fortitude; and 4. Temperance.

'They are called *Cardinal* Virtues because they are, as it were, the hinges (*cardines*) by which the whole moral life of a Christian is supported, and on which it must constantly move.'

*474. What is *Prudence?*

Prudence teaches us not only to know and to will what is right, but also to choose the proper means.

. . . 'Prove what is the good, and the acceptable, and the perfect will of God' (Rom. xii. 2).

*475. What is *Justice?*

Justice disposes us always to do what is right and to give to every one his due.

'Render to Cæsar the things that are Cæsar's, and to God the things that are God's' (Matt. xxii. 21).

*476. What is *Fortitude?*

Fortitude gives us courage to suffer anything rather than fail in our duty.

Example: The seven Machabees and their mother, who esteemed torments as nothing (2 Mac. vii. 12).

*477. What is *Temperance?*

Temperance subdues those inclinations and desires which may lead to evil.

'Refrain yourselves from carnal desires, which war against the soul' (1 Pet. ii. 11).

*478. What Virtues are opposite to the seven Capital Sins?

These seven: 1. Humility; 2. Liberality; 3. Chastity; 4. Meekness; 5. Temperance in eating and drinking; 6. Brotherly Love; 7. Diligence.

Application: Unless you persevere in the struggle with your wicked inclinations, you will not acquire the Christian Virtues; therefore fight faithfully until death and God will give you the crown of life (Apoc. ii. 10).

*§ 2. *On Christian Perfection.*

479. In what does Christian Perfection consist?

Christian Perfection consists in freedom from all inordinate or excessive love of the world and of ourselves, so that we may love God above all, and all things in God.

'What have I in Heaven? and besides Thee what do I desire upon earth? Thou art the God of my heart, and the God that is my portion for ever' (Psalms lxxii. 25, 26).

480. Which is the best way to Perfection?

The imitation of Jesus Christ.

'If thou wilt be perfect, . . . and come, follow me' (Matt. xix. 21).

481. What particular means has Jesus Christ recommended for attaining perfection?

Chiefly those called the *Evangelical Counsels.*

482. Which are the Evangelical Counsels?

The Evangelical Counsels are, 1. Voluntary Poverty; 2. Perpetual Chastity; and 3. Entire Obedience to a Spiritual Superior.

483. Who are obliged to observe the Evangelical Counsels?
All Religious, and all those who have bound themselves by vow to keep them.

484. Can people in the world lead a perfect life?
Yes, if they live not according to the spirit of the world, but according to the spirit of Jesus Christ.

He said to all: 'Be ye therefore perfect, as also your Heavenly Father is perfect' (Matt. v. 48).

485. But is the spirit of the world opposed to the spirit of Christ?
Most certainly it is, as we see from those sentences of our Saviour called the *Eight Beatitudes*.

486. Which are the Eight Beatitudes?
1. 'Blessed are the poor in spirit; for theirs is the kingdom of Heaven.
2. Blessed are the meek; for they shall possess the land.
3. Blessed are they that mourn; for they shall be comforted.
4. Blessed are they that hunger and thirst after justice; for they shall have their fill.
5. Blessed are the merciful; for they shall obtain mercy.
6. Blessed are the clean of heart; for they shall see God.
7. Blessed are the peacemakers; for they shall be called the children of God.
8. Blessed are they that suffer persecution for justice' sake; for theirs is the kingdom of Heaven' (Matt. v. 3–10).

487. How do we know that the spirit of the world is opposed to the spirit of Christ?
We know it because the world calls those very persons foolish and miserable whom our Lord calls blessed.

488. What must we do to attain to Perfection?

To attain to Perfection we must, 1. Take delight in and attentively hear the Word of God, and often receive the Holy Sacraments; 2. We must constantly deny ourselves; and 3. We must perform our daily actions in the state of grace and in a manner pleasing to God.

489. How should we deny ourselves?

We should deny ourselves many things that are pleasant to us, even lawful things, so as the more easily to abstain from unlawful things.

490. How may we perform our daily actions in a manner pleasing to God?

By keeping the life of Jesus Christ in our mind, and striving to imitate Him.

491. How should we do our daily work?

After the example of Christ—industriously, cheerfully, and according to the will of God.

492. What should we do at meal-time?

We should say grace reverently and devoutly before and after meals, and be temperate and modest at the table.

493. How should we act under affliction?

We should remember that affliction comes from God, and we should offer it to Him, and beg of Him the grace to make a good use of it.

Application: Think that these words, which God spoke to Abraham, are addressed also to you: 'Walk before me, and be perfect' (Gen. xvii. 1). Strive earnestly to become more and more pious and virtuous. 'My son, serve God with a perfect heart and a willing mind; for the Lord searcheth all hearts, and understandeth all the thoughts of minds. If thou seek Him, thou shalt find Him; but if thou forsake Him, He will cast thee off forever' (1 Par. xxviii. 9).

PART III.

ON THE MEANS OF GRACE.

Grace in General.

494. Can we by our own strength keep the Commandments and be saved?

No, we cannot, without the grace of God.

'Without me you can do nothing,' says Christ (John. xv. 5).

495. What do we mean by the grace of God?

By the grace of God we mean an interior supernatural help or gift which God confers upon us, through the merits of Jesus Christ, for our eternal salvation.

496. How many kinds of grace are there?

There are two kinds: 1. The *grace of assistance*, called also *actual* grace; and 2. The *grace of sanctification*, called also *sanctifying* grace or *habitual* grace.

§ 1. *On the Grace of Assistance.*

497. In what does Actual Grace consist?

Actual Grace consists in this: that God enlightens our understanding, and inclines our will to avoid evil and to desire and to do what is good.

498. Is Actual Grace necessary?

Actual Grace is so necessary that without it we cannot begin, continue, or accomplish the least thing towards our salvation.

'For it is God who worketh in you both to will and to accomplish' (Philip ii. 13).

499. Does God give His grace to all men?

Yes; God gives to all men sufficient grace to work out their salvation.

'God will have all men to be saved, and to come to the knowledge of the truth' (1. Tim. ii. 4).

500. What must we do that the grace of God may lead to our salvation?

We must not resist it, but faithfully co-operate with it.

'We exhort you, that you receive not the grace of God in vain' (2 Cor. vi. 1).

501. Can we resist the grace of God?

We can; for God's grace does not force our will, but leaves it perfectly free.

'To-day, if you shall hear his voice, harden not your hearts' (Ps. xciv. 8).

Application: Pray daily for the grace of God, and be careful not to close your heart against it.

§ 2. *The Grace of Sanctification.*

502. What is Sanctifying Grace?

Sanctifying Grace is an unmerited supernatural gift which the Holy Ghost imparts to our souls, and which renders us just, children of God, and heirs of Heaven.

503. Why is sanctifying grace an unmerited gift?

Because it is a free gift coming from the pitying love of God.

'For all have sinned, and do need the glory of God; being justified freely [*i.e.*, without their desert] by His grace through the redemption that is in Christ Jesus' (Rom. iii. 23, 24).

*504. Why is sanctifying grace also called 'Justifying Grace'?

Because by sanctifying grace we are justified—that is, we are brought from sin to the state of righteousness and holiness.

505. Where does the sinner receive sanctifying grace?

First in the Sacrament of Baptism; and if he has lost it, he recovers it in the Sacrament of Penance.

506. How long does sanctifying grace remain in the soul?

As long as we are free from mortal sin.

507. What fruits does the just man produce by the help of grace?

He produces good, or meritorious, works: 'For every good tree bringeth forth good fruit' (Matt. vii. 17).

*508. Can one who is in mortal sin do good?

He can do good, but cannot merit Heaven (John xv. 4, 5).

*509. Is it useless, then, to do good when in mortal sin?

On the contrary, it is very useful for obtaining from God's mercy the grace of conversion, and sometimes for averting temporal punishment.

Example: The Ninivites.

510. What do we merit by good works done in the state of grace?

We merit, 1. An increase of sanctifying grace; and 2. Eternal salvation.

511. Whence do our good works derive their merit?

From the infinite merits of Jesus Christ, whose living members we are through sanctifying grace (John xv. 5).

512. Must every Christian perform good works?

Yes, for 'every tree that doth not yield good

fruit shall be cut down, and cast into the fire' (Matt. iii. 10).

*513. What good works are especially recommended in Holy Scripture?

The Scriptures specially recommend prayer, fasting, and alms, by which in general are understood works of devotion, mortification, and charity.

'Prayer is good with fasting and alms, more than to lay up treasures of gold' (Tob. xii. 8).

514. What does God most consider in our good works?

Our good intention, through which we may merit from God great reward for even small works.

515. What is good intention?

Good intention is the desire, or act of the will, to serve God and to honor Him.

516. How may we briefly form a good intention?

We may say, 'My Lord and my God, all for Thy honor.'

517. When should we form a good intention?

It is useful to form a good intention often during the day, and especially in the morning.

518. What principal means have we to obtain grace?

The Holy Sacraments and Prayer.

Application: Strive most carefully to preserve sanctifying grace always in your heart by avoiding sin and performing good works.

THE SACRAMENTS.

519. What is a Sacrament?

A Sacrament is a visible sign, instituted by Jesus Christ, through which invisible grace and sanctification are communicated to our souls.

520. What constitutes a Sacrament?

Three things: 1. A visible sign; 2. An invisible grace; and 3. Institution by Jesus Christ.

521. What graces do the Sacraments confer?

1. The Sacraments either communicate or increase sanctifying grace; and 2. Each Sacrament communicates peculiar graces suited to the end for which it was instituted.

522. How must we receive the Sacraments in order to obtain their graces?

We must prepare ourselves well for them, and then receive them worthily.

523. What sin does he commit who receives a Sacrament unworthily?

He commits a very grievous sin—a sacrilege.

524. Do the Sacraments depend for their efficacy upon the worthiness of those who administer them?

No; the Sacraments have their efficacy from the infinite merits of Jesus Christ, by whom they were instituted.

525. How many Sacraments did Christ institute?

These seven: 1. Baptism; 2. Confirmation; 3. Holy Eucharist; 4. Penance; 5. Extreme Unction; 6. Holy Orders; and 7. Matrimony.

526. How do we know that there are seven Sacraments?

We know it because the Church, 'which is the pillar and ground of the truth' (1 Tim. iii. 15), has at all times taught and used these seven.

*527. How are the Sacraments divided?

They are divided, 1. Into Sacraments of the *living* and Sacraments of the *dead;* and 2. Into such as can be received only *once*, and such as can be received *more than once*.

*528. Which are the Sacraments of the living?

The Sacraments of the *living* are: 1. Confirmation; 2. Holy Eucharist; 3. Extreme Unction; 4. Holy Orders; and 5. Matrimony.

*529. Why are they called Sacraments of the *living?*

Because to receive them we should have supernatural life—that is to say, sanctifying grace.

*530. Which are the Sacraments of the dead?

The Sacraments of the dead are Baptism and Penance.

*531. Why are they called Sacraments of the dead?

Because to receive them we either have not, or are not required to have, the life of grace.

*532. Which Sacraments can be received only once?

Baptism, Confirmation, and Holy Orders.

*533. Why can they be received only once?

Because they imprint upon the soul an indelible mark.

Application: Thank God with your whole heart for the precious Sacraments, and beware of profaning them by disrespectful language or by unworthily receiving them.

BAPTISM.

534. Which is the first and most necessary Sacrament?

The first and most necessary Sacrament is Baptism.

535. Why is Baptism the first Sacrament?

Because before Baptism no other Sacrament can be validly received.

536. Why is Baptism the most necessary Sacrament?

Because without Baptism no one can be saved.

'Unless a man be born again of water and the Holy Ghost, he cannot enter into the kingdom of God' (John iii. 5).

537. What is Baptism?

Baptism is a Sacrament in which, by water and

the word of God, we are cleansed from all sin, and regenerated and sanctified in Christ to life everlasting.

*538. Why do we say that we are baptized '*by water and the word of God*'?

Because Baptism is administered by pouring water over the head or over the body of him who is to be baptized, and at the same time pronouncing the words, 'I baptize thee in the name of the Father, and of the Son, and of the Holy Ghost.'

*539. Why do we say that '*in Baptism we are cleansed from all sin*'?

Because in Baptism original sin, and all other sins committed before Baptism, are forgiven.

540. And is the punishment due to sin remitted?

Yes; the temporal as well as the eternal punishment is remitted in Baptism.

*541. And why do we say that we are '*regenerated and sanctified to life everlasting*'?

Because in Baptism we are not only cleansed from all sin, but are also transformed in a spiritual manner, and are made holy, children of God, and heirs of Heaven.

*542. How is this regeneration and sanctification effected?

It is effected by sanctifying grace, through which the Holy Ghost infuses the Theological Virtues into the soul.

'The charity of God is poured forth into our hearts by the Holy Ghost, who is given us' (Rom. v. 5).

*543. And why do we say that we are regenerated and sanctified '*in Christ*'?

To signify that in Baptism all these graces are given us, because we are there united to Christ and incorporated with His Church.

*544. Who can validly baptize?

Any person; but, except in case of necessity, none are allowed to baptize but priests who have care of souls.

*545. What sort of water should be used for Baptism?

Any natural water will do for the validity of Baptism. But, when possible, baptismal water, blessed for the purpose, should be used.

*546. What intention must he have who baptizes?

He must have the intention really to baptize—that is, to do what the Church does or what Christ has ordained.

*547. What vows do we make in Baptism?

These vows: 1. To believe firmly and always the doctrines of the Catholic Church; 2. To shun sin and all occasions of evil; and 3. To live a pious life.

*548. What must sponsors, or godfathers and godmothers, bear in mind?

They should bear in mind that they become the spiritual parents of the infant to be baptized, and that they make the baptismal vows in its name, and therefore, 1. Should be good Catholics themselves; 2. If the infant lose its parents they should see that it is instructed in the Catholic religion, and properly brought up according to its station in life; and 3. They cannot marry their godchild or its parents.

*549. Can nothing supply the place of Baptism by water?

When Baptism by water cannot be had it may be replaced by the Baptism of desire or by the Baptism of blood.

*550. What is the Baptism of desire?

Baptism of desire is an earnest wish to receive

Baptism, accompanied with a perfect contrition or a pure love of God.

*551. What is the Baptism of blood?
Martyrdom for the sake of Christ.

Application: Never forget what you owe to God for the priceless grace of Baptism, and what the Priest said when he put the white garment upon you: 'Receive this white garment, and bring it unspotted before the judgment-seat of our Lord Jesus Christ, that thou mayest obtain life everlasting.' Renew your Baptismal vows often —every Sunday, if possible.

Confirmation.

552. What is Confirmation?
Confirmation is a Sacrament in which, through the laying on of the Bishop's hands, anointing, and prayer, those who have been baptized are strengthened by the Holy Ghost, in order that they may steadfastly profess their faith and piously live up to it.

Example: The Apostles Peter and John went into Samaria, and there confirmed those who had been already baptized (Acts viii.)

553. What are the effects of Confirmation?
1. Confirmation increases sanctifying grace; 2. In it the Holy Ghost comes to help us to fight against evil and to grow in virtue; and 3. It imprints an indelible spiritual mark upon us as soldiers of Christ.

554. Who has power to confirm?
The power to confirm belongs to the Bishops as successors of the Apostles.

555. How does the Bishop give Confirmation?
The Bishop spreads his hands over those to be confirmed, and prays the Holy Ghost to descend upon them; and then he lays his hand upon each one, and anoints him with holy chrism; and he

concludes by giving them the Episcopal Benediction.

556. How does the Bishop anoint those to be confirmed?

He makes the sign of the Cross with chrism upon the forehead of each one, saying at the same time: 'I sign thee with the sign of the Cross, and I confirm thee with the chrism of salvation, in the name of the Father, and of the Son, and of the Holy Ghost.'

557. Of what does the chrism consist?

Of oil of olives and balsam.

558. What does the oil signify?

The oil signifies inward strength for the combat with the enemies of our salvation.

559. Why is fragrant balsam mixed with the oil?

Fragrant balsam is mixed with the oil to signify that he who is confirmed receives the grace to keep himself clean from the corruption of the world, and to give forth the sweet odor of virtue by leading a pious life.

560. Why does the Bishop make the sign of the Cross on the forehead of him whom he confirms?

To teach us that a Christian must never be ashamed of the Cross, but boldly profess his faith in Jesus crucified.

'I am not ashamed of the Gospel; for it is the power of God unto salvation to every one that believeth' (Rom. i. 16).

561. Why does the Bishop, after anointing him, give him a slight blow on the cheek?

To remind him that, as he is now strengthened, he should be ready to suffer patiently any humiliation for the name of Jesus.

562. Is Confirmation necessary to salvation?

Confirmation is not necessary to salvation; yet it

would be sinful to neglect receiving it out of indifference.

563. Who can receive Confirmation?
Every one who is baptized.

564. How is one to receive Confirmation?
1. One should be in the state of grace, and should pray devoutly for the gift of the Holy Ghost; 2. He should promise God to live and die a good Christian; 3. He should not leave the church before the Bishop has given his benediction.

565. What is required of the sponsors in Confirmation?
They must be Catholics, must have been confirmed, and should encourage those for whom they stand by deed and word.

Application: Perform without fear all the duties of a Catholic Christian.

The Holy Eucharist.

§ 1. *The Real Presence of Christ in the Blessed Sacrament.*

566. What is the Holy Eucharist?
It is the true Body and the true Blood of our Lord Jesus Christ, who is really and substantially present under the appearances of bread and wine for the nourishment of our souls.

It is called Eucharist from the Greek word *Eucharistia*, which means *Good Grace*.

567. Are all the essentials of a Sacrament in the Holy Eucharist?
Yes; there are, 1. The visible sign—that is, the appearances of bread and wine; 2. The invisible grace, which is Jesus Christ Himself, the Author and Dispenser of all graces; and 3. The institution by Jesus Christ.

568. When did Jesus Christ institute this Sacrament?

He instituted it at the Last Supper the evening before His bitter Passion.

*569. How did He institute it?

Jesus took bread, blessed it, and broke and gave it to His Disciples, saying: '*Take ye and eat; this is my Body.*' After that, in like manner, He took the chalice with wine in it, blessed and gave it to His Disciples, saying: '*Drink ye all of this; this is my Blood.*'

'Do this for a commemoration of me' (Short Hist. of Rel., § 24).

*570. What became of the bread and wine when Jesus pronounced the words, 'This is my Body; this is my Blood'?

The bread was changed into the true Body, and the wine into the true Blood, of Jesus Christ?

*571. What then remained of the bread and wine?

Nothing but their appearances.

*572. What is meant by the appearances of bread and wine?

All that our senses perceive of bread and wine—as form, color, taste, etc.

*573. How do we know that with the words, 'This is my Body; this is my Blood,' Christ gave His true Body and His true Blood to His Apostles?

We know it, 1. Because Christ had long before promised to His Disciples that He would give them His real Flesh to eat and His real Blood to drink,* and then, at the Last Supper, He plainly

---

* 'The bread that I will give is my flesh for the life of the world. The Jews, therefore, strove among themselves, saying: How can this man give us His flesh to eat? Then Jesus said to them: Amen, amen, I say

declared that what He then gave them as food and drink was really His Body and His Blood; and 2. Because the Apostles and the Catholic Church have ever believed and taught so.*

*574. Did Christ give His Apostles this power of changing bread and wine into His sacred Flesh and Blood?

Yes; He gave them this power with the words, 'Do this for a commemoration of me.'

*575. To whom did this power pass from the Apostles?

It passed from the Apostles to the Bishops and Priests.

*576. When do the Bishops and Priests exercise this power.

At Mass, when they pronounce over the bread and wine these words: 'This is my Body, this is my Blood.'

*577. Is there, then, no bread and wine on the altar after the consecration?

No; there is then on the altar the true Body and the true Blood of Jesus Christ, under the appearances of bread and wine.

578. How long does Christ remain present with His sacred Flesh and Blood?

As long as the appearances of bread and wine continue.

579. Is the Body of Christ alone present under

unto you: Except you eat the flesh of the Son of man, and drink His blood, you shall not have life in you. For my flesh is meat indeed, and my blood is drink indeed' (John vi. 52, etc.)

* The teaching of the Apostles, especially of St. Paul, is evident from 1 Cor. x. 16 and xi. 23-29; and the teaching of the whole Church from the beginning is shown from her prayers and rites relating to the Divine Service; from the decrees of her Councils; and from the numerous testimonies of the holy Fathers and ecclesiastical writers.

the appearance of bread, and the Blood of Christ alone present under the appearance of wine?

No; under each appearance Christ is present entire and undivided, as He is entire and undivided in Heaven.

580. When the Priest breaks or divides the Sacred Host, does he also break the Body of Christ?

No; he breaks or divides the appearances only. The entire and living body of Christ is present in each part in a true though mysterious manner.

581. What does the Real Presence of Jesus Christ in the Blessed Sacrament require us to do?

To visit Him often, and to adore Him with the deepest humility and the warmest love.

582. What other reasons are there for the real Presence of Christ.

He is present for two other reasons 1. That He may offer Himself for us in the *Holy Sacrifice of the Mass;* and 2. That in *Holy Communion* He may give Himself to us for the nourishment of our souls.

Application: Be always respectful and devout when in church, where our Lord and Saviour is pleased to be present. Go there often to adore Him and implore His grace.

§ 2. *The Holy Sacrifice of the Mass.*

583. What is a Sacrifice?

A Sacrifice is that first and highest act of Religion in which a duly authorized person offers to God some sensible thing which is visibly immolated either physically or mystically, in token and acknowledgment of God's supreme dominion over all things and of our total dependence on Him.

He who sacrifices is styled a *priest;* the sensible thing which is sacrificed is called the *victim;* the place where it is sacrificed is the *altar.* These four—*priest, victim, altar*, and *sacrifice*—are inseparable. Each one of them calls for the others.

*584. Have Sacrifices always been offered?

Yes, Sacrifices have been offered from the beginning of the world, and under the Old Law they were commanded by God Himself.

*585. Why were the Sacrifices of the Old Law abolished?

Because they were only symbols of the unspotted Sacrifice of the New Law, and were therefore not to last longer than the Old Law itself.

*586. Which is the Sacrifice of the New Law?

The Son of God Himself, Jesus Christ, who, by His death on the Cross, offered Himself to His Heavenly Father for us (Heb. ix. 14).

*587. Was all Sacrifice to cease with the death of Christ?

No; in the New Law of Grace there was to be a *Perpetual Sacrifice*, as God had promised by the Prophet Malachy.

'From the rising of the sun even to the going down my name is great among the Gentiles, and in every place there is Sacrifice, and there is offered to my name a clean oblation' (Mal. i. 10, 11).

*588. What is this perpetual Sacrifice foretold by Malachy?

It is the Sacrifice of the Mass.

589. Who instituted the Sacrifice of the Mass?

Jesus Christ instituted the Sacrifice of the Mass at the Last Supper.

590. What is the Mass?

The Mass is the perpetual Sacrifice of the New Law in which Christ our Lord offers Himself to His Heavenly Father, under the appearances of bread and wine, by the hands of the Priest, in an unbloody manner, as He once offered Himself on the Cross in a bloody manner.

*591. What is the difference between the Sacrifice of the Mass and the Sacrifice of the Cross?

The Sacrifice of the Mass is essentially the same as that of the Cross, but the manner of offering is different.

*592. Why is the Sacrifice of the Mass the same as that of the Cross?

Because in both the same Victim is offered— Jesus Christ our Lord.

*593. How is the manner of offering different in both?

On the Cross Christ offered Himself for us in a bloody manner, while in the Mass He offers Himself in an unbloody manner.

NOTE: On the Cross Christ died. In the Mass He does not die, but His death on the Cross is mystically represented by the apparent separation of the Body and the Blood under the distinct appearances of the bread and of the wine.

594. What are the parts of the Mass?

The principal parts of the Mass are, 1. The Offertory; 2. The Consecration; and 3. The Communion.

*595. To whom do we offer the Sacrifice of the Mass?

We offer it to God alone; but we also celebrate in it the memory of the Saints.

*596. How do we celebrate the memory of the Saints in the Mass?

1. By thanking God for the grace and salvation bestowed upon them; and 2. By asking their intercession for us.

597. For what ends do we offer the Mass to God?

We offer it to God, 1. As a *Sacrifice of Praise* for His honor and glory; 2. As a *Sacrifice of Thanksgiving* for all the graces and benefits received from Him; 3. As a *Sacrifice of Propitiation* for our many offences against Him; and 4. As a *Sacrifice of Prayer* to obtain His assistance in all our needs of soul and body.

*598. To whom are the fruits of the Mass applied?

To the whole Church, both to the living and to the dead.

Application: Assist at the Holy Sacrifice of the Mass with sincere devotion and with great reverence, and try to hear Mass every day. At the Offertory offer yourself with Jesus Christ to your Heavenly Father; at the Consecration humbly adore your Saviour and beg His pardon; at the Communion communicate, at least *spiritually*—that is to say, desire earnestly to be united with your dear Lord in this Sacrament of Love.

*§ 3. *Holy Communion.*

599. What is Holy Communion?

Holy Communion is the actual receiving of the real Body and Blood of Jesus Christ for the nourishment of the soul.

600. Who has commanded us to receive Holy Communion?

God has commanded it, as well as the Church. For Christ our Lord says plainly: 'Amen, amen, I say unto you, except you eat the Flesh of the Son of man, and drink His Blood, you shall not have life in you' (John vi. 54).

601. Must we drink of the chalice in order to partake of the Blood of Christ?

No; for the Blood of Christ cannot be separated from His Body, and under the appearance of the bread we receive His Body and His Blood.

602. Why, then, did Christ institute the Holy Eucharist under both kinds?

Because He instituted it not merely as a Sacrament but also as a Sacrifice, for which both kinds are necessary.

603. What graces does Holy Communion impart to us?

1. It unites us most closely to Christ and increases sanctifying grace; 2. It weakens our evil inclinations and makes us able and eager to do good; 3. It cleanses us from venial sin and preserves us from mortal sin; 4. It is a pledge of our resurrection and everlasting salvation.

604. Does every one receive graces in Holy Communion?

No; whoever receives Holy Communion unworthily—that is, in mortal sin—brings damnation upon himself.

'Whoever shall eat this Bread or drink the Chalice of the Lord unworthily shall be guilty of the Body and of the Blood of the Lord. But let a man prove himself, and so let him eat of that Bread, and drink of the Chalice; for he that eateth and drinketh unworthily, eateth and drinketh judgment to himself, not discerning the Body of the Lord' (1 Cor. xi. 27-29). Comparison with the Ark of the Covenant, which brought happiness and blessing upon the pious Israelites, but misfortune and a curse upon the impious Philistines.

605. What sin does he commit who communicates unworthily?

Like Judas, he commits a horrible sacrilege.

606. What must we do when we have committed a grievous sin?

We must make a good confession before we receive.

'Let a man prove himself, and so let him eat of that Bread' (1 Cor. xi. 28).

607. What other preparation must we make for Holy Communion?

We must try, 1. To cleanse our soul from venial sin also; and 2. Excite ourselves to fervor and devotion.

608. Does venial sin render our Communions unworthy?

Venial sin does not render them unworthy or sacrilegious, but it lessens the graces which we would otherwise receive.

609. How can we excite ourselves to fervor and devotion?

By pious meditation and devout exercises.

610. Which are the best exercises before Holy Communion?

The Acts, 1. Of Faith and Adoration; 2. Of Humility and Contrition; and 3. Of Hope, Love, and ardent Desire.

611. How must we prepare ourselves as to the *body*?

1. We must be fasting—that is, we must not have eaten or drunk the least thing from twelve o'clock the night before; and 2. We must be decently dressed.

612. Who are dispensed from the obligation of fasting at such a time?

Those who are dangerously ill and receive the Blessed Sacrament as a *Viaticum*—that is to say, as a preparation for their last journey.

613. How should we approach the altar-rail?

With the greatest reverence, with hands joined and downcast eyes.

614. What should we do at the time of receiving the Sacred Host?

We should spread the communion-cloth under the chin, throw back the head, put out the tongue and extend it a little upon the lower lip, and then most reverently receive the Sacred Host.

Do not keep the Sacred Host in your mouth until it is quite dissolved; but let it moisten a little upon your tongue, and then swallow it. Should it stick to the roof of your mouth, remove it with your tongue, and not with your finger.

615. What should we do after receiving Holy Communion?

We should retire with the greatest modesty to our place, and spend some time in devout prayer.

616. What sort of prayers ought we especially to say after Holy Communion?

Those in which we humble ourselves before the Lord, thank Him, offer ourselves up to Him, express our love, and implore His graces.

617. How should we spend the day of Communion?

We should spend it as much as possible in pious exercises, and avoid worldly recreations and amusements.

Application: Resolve to approach the Holy Table as often as is permitted, and receive the Bread of Angels with as much devotion and purity of heart as you can attain.

Penance.

618. What is the Sacrament of Penance?

It is a Sacrament in which the Priest, as God's representative, forgives sins, when the sinner is heartily sorry for them, sincerely confesses them, and is willing to do penance for them.

619. Does the Priest really forgive the sins, or does he only declare them forgiven?

The priest really and truly forgives sins through the power given him by Christ.

620. When did Christ give the power of forgiving sins?

When after His resurrection He breathed upon the Apostles and said to them: 'Receive ye the Holy Ghost. Whose sins you shall forgive, they are forgiven them, and whose sins you shall retain, they are retained' (John xx. 22, 23).

621. Did Christ impart this power to the Apostles alone?

No; He imparted it to all their successors in the priesthood also, as the Church has always believed and taught.

622. Why was the power of forgiving sins to pass from the Apostles to their successors?

Because Christ instituted His means of salvation for all times and all men.

623. Can all sins be forgiven in the Sacrament of Penance?

Yes; all sins committed after Baptism can be forgiven, if we confess them with the right disposition of repentance.

'If we confess our sins, He is faithful and just to forgive us our sins, and to cleanse us from all iniquity' (1 John i. 9).

624. Why must we confess our sins in order to be forgiven?

Because Christ so ordained when He instituted the Sacrament of Penance.

625. How do we prove that Christ ordained Confession?

We prove it by His own words, 'Whose sins you shall forgive,' etc., for unless we make known our sins to the Priest, he cannot judge whether to forgive or to retain them.

626. Is the Sacrament of Penance necessary for salvation to all who have sinned?

It is necessary for salvation to all who have committed grievous sin after Baptism.

627. Can sin be forgiven without the Sacrament of Penance?

When the Sacrament of Penance cannot be

received it can be supplied by a perfect contrition and a firm resolve to confess as soon as possible.

628. What does God do for us through the Sacrament of Penance?

1. He forgives sins committed after Baptism; 2. He remits the eternal and a part of the temporal punishment due for our sins; 3. He restores sanctifying grace, or, if not lost, increases it; and 4. He confers other graces to enable us to lead a holy life.

629. How many things are necessary to receive the Sacrament of Penance worthily?

These five: 1. Examination of Conscience; 2. Contrition; 3. Resolution of Amendment; 4. Confession; and 5. Satisfaction, or Penance.

§ 1. *Examination of Conscience.*

630. What do we mean by *Examination of Conscience?*

Examination of conscience is a serious meditation upon our sins in order to know them well.

631. How must we begin the Examination of Conscience?

We must begin by imploring the Holy Ghost to give us the grace to know, to repent, and to confess our sins.

632. How may we implore the Holy Ghost for this grace?

Come, O Holy Ghost! enlighten my understanding, that I may rightly know my sins; and move my heart, that I may properly repent of them, sincerely confess them, and truly amend my life.

633. How should we examine our conscience?

1. We should find out when we last made a good Confession and whether we performed the

penance given us; and 2. We should go through the Commandments of God and of the Church, our duties in life, and the different kinds of sin, so as to know how we have offended God in thought, word, deed, and omission.

634. How may children easily remember their sins?

By considering how they have behaved in church, in school, at home towards their parents, brothers, and sisters, in the street or at work, when alone or in company.

635. Must we examine as to the number and circumstances of our sins?

Yes; at least when they are mortal.

636. What faults should we guard against in examining our conscience?

1. We must not examine ourselves too hastily or slightly; 2. We must not skip our favorite sins; and 3. We must avoid becoming too scrupulous.

637. How can we make our examination easy?

By examining our conscience every day, and by going to Confession often.

§ 2. *Contrition.*

638. What is Contrition?

Contrition is a hearty sorrow for our sins and a hatred of them.

Example: 'Peter went out and wept bitterly' (Matt. xxvi. 75).

639. What qualities must Contrition have?

It must be, 1. Interior; 2. Universal; and 3. Supernatural.

640. How must Contrition be *interior?*

We must grieve for our sins not merely in words, but we must also hate them in our heart as the greatest evil, and sincerely wish we had not committed them.

'A sacrifice to God is an afflicted spirit; a contrite and humble heart, O God, Thou wilt not despise' (Ps. 1. 19).

641. How must Contrition be *general?*

We must be sorry for *all* the mortal sins we have committed.

642. Is our confession valid if we have no sorrow for our venial sins?

If we have only venial sins to confess, and are not sorry for any of them, our confession is null.

643. How must Contrition be *supernatural?*

We must grieve for our sins not merely because of the temporal trouble they bring us, but because they offend God, deprive us of His grace, deserve Hell, and call for punishment from God.

644. Why is it not enough to be sorry for our sins on account of the temporal trouble they bring us?

Because to be sorry for sin only because through it we have lost health, property, reputation, etc., is nothing but natural sorrow, which does not avail for everlasting life.

Thus the sorrow of King Saul, Antiochus, and others was a merely natural sorrow; on the contrary, that of King David, Mary Magdalen, Zacheus, the Apostles Peter and Paul, and other Scripture penitents, was supernatural.

645. What should we do to obtain supernatural Contrition?

We should, 1. Earnestly ask God for His grace; and 2. Seriously think on what Faith teaches us of the wickedness of sin and its evil consequences.

646. How many kinds of supernatural Contrition are there?

There are two kinds, *Perfect* Contrition and *Imperfect* Contrition.

647. When is Contrition *perfect*?

Contrition is *perfect* when, out of a perfect love of God, we hate sin more than all other evils, because it offends God, who is the Supreme Good.

648. When is Contrition *imperfect*?

When our love is not perfect, and when, therefore, our fear of Hell and of the loss of Heaven, or our sense of the heinousness of sin itself, must unite with it in causing us to detest sin above all other evils, and to resolve to offend God no more.

649. Is *Perfect* Contrition necessary?

Perfect Contrition is not necessary for Confession, but yet we should strive to obtain it.

*650. Why should we strive to obtain Perfect Contrition?

Because the more perfect our Contrition, the more meritorious and the more pleasing to God is our repentance, and the more certain will be our forgiveness.

651. When should we make an Act of Perfect Contrition, outside of Confession?

1. When in danger of death; and 2. As often as we commit a mortal sin and cannot go to Confession at once.

652. When must we make the Act of Contrition in the Sacrament of Penance?

We must make it before our Confession, or at least before the Priest gives us Absolution.

653. Can we obtain forgiveness without Contrition in case of necessity?

No; Contrition is so necessary that nothing can supply its place.

§ 3. *Purpose of Amendment.*

654. What must be joined with Contrition?

With Contrition there must be joined, 1. Hope of forgiveness; and 2. Purpose of Amendment.

655. What is a Purpose of Amendment?

A Purpose of Amendment is a sincere resolution to amend our life and to sin no more.

656. What qualities must a Purpose of Amendment have?

Like Contrition, a Purpose of Amendment must be, 1. Interior or Sincere; 2. General; and 3. Supernatural.

657. How do we form a Purpose of Amendment?

We resolve, 1. To avoid at least all grievous sins and the proximate occasion of sin; 2. To use the necessary means of amendment; and 3. To make satisfaction for our sins, and repair whatever harm we may have done our neighbor.

658. What means the *proximate occasion of sin?*

Proximate occasion of sin means a person, company, amusement, or whatever else has caused us to sin before, and is likely to do so again, unless avoided.

659. What of those who will not avoid the proximate occasion, or will not give up their habitual sins?

The Priest's Absolution is of no use to them, but only increases their guilt.

660. How can we make an Act of Contrition, with a Resolution of Amendment, before going to Confession?

In this manner: O my God! from the bottom of my heart I am sorry for all my sins; not only because by them I have rendered myself unworthy of Thy grace, and liable to Thy just punishment in this life and in the next, but especially because I have offended Thee, the Sovereign, Most Perfect, and Most Amiable Good, whom I now love above all things. I hate and detest all my sins, and am firmly resolved never more to offend Thee, my most amiable God, and carefully to avoid the occasion of sin.

§ 4. *Confession.*

661. What is Confession?

Confession is the sorrowful accusation of our sins to a Priest, in order that we may obtain absolution from him.

662. What qualities are necessary for Confession?

Confession must be, 1. Complete; 2. Sincere; and 3. Clear.

663. When is Confession complete?

Confession is complete when we confess at least all the mortal sins that we remember, as well as their number and circumstances.

664. What must we do if we cannot recall their number?

We must tell the number as nearly as we can, and declare about how often in a day, week, or month we have committed the sin.

665. What circumstances must we confess?

Every circumstance, 1. That might make a mortal sin of a venial one; or 2. That might change a mortal sin into one of a different kind; for example, a theft into a sacrilege.

666. What must we avoid in Confession?

We must avoid making known those who have been concerned in our sins, and we must express ourselves as modestly as possible.

667. Must we confess venial sins also?

We are not bound to confess venial sins, but it is well to do so.

668. What must we do if in doubt whether a sin is mortal or venial?

We should confess what we are in doubt about, because many mistake mortal sins for venial ones.

669. When is Confession sincere?

Confession is sincere when we frankly accuse ourselves just as we are guilty before God, without disguise or excuse.

670. What should he do who is ashamed to confess?

He should consider, 1. That a Confession which is not sincere is sacrilegious and merits eternal damnation; and 2. That it is better to confess his sins to a Priest, who will not betray them, than to live unhappily in sin, and on the last day to be put to shame before the whole world.

*671. What must we do if we have omitted a sin which we were bound to confess?

1. If we have omitted any sin through forgetfulness, we must accuse ourselves of it in our next confession; 2. If we have omitted any sin through shame or through carelessness, the confession must be all repeated, and we must accuse ourselves of this omission.

672. When is Confession clear?

Confession is clear when we accuse ourselves in plain language, so that the Confessor can see the state of our conscience.

*673. What is a General Confession?

A General Confession is one in which we repeat some or all of our former Confessions.

*674. When is a General Confession necessary?

Whenever a former Confession was useless through want of sincerity, sorrow, purpose of amendment, or of care in the examination of our conscience.

675. How do you begin your Confession?

Having made the sign of the Cross, I say: 'I, a poor and miserable sinner, accuse myself to God, the Almighty, and to you, my Father, in His stead, that since my last Confession, which was . . . I have committed the following sins.' (Here I confess my sins.)

Or in the following manner:
Having arrived at the Confessional, I kneel down, make the sign of the Cross, and ask the Priest's blessing by saying: 'Bless me, Father, for I have sinned.' After receiving his blessing I say the first part of the *Confiteor* as far as 'through my most grievous fault.' Then I say how long it is since my last Confession, whether I then received Absolution and performed my Penance. After this I confess all the sins I can recollect, beginning with those which I may have forgotten in my last Confession.

676. How do you end your Confession?

In conclusion I say: 'For these, and all the sins of my whole life, I am most heartily sorry, because by them I have offended God, the Supreme and Most Amiable Good. I detest all my sins, and am firmly resolved to amend my life and to sin no more. I humbly ask Penance and Absolution of you, my Ghostly Father.'

Or I conclude by saying: 'For these, and all my other sins which I cannot at present call to my remembrance, and also for the sins of my past life, especially for . . . I am heartily sorry, purpose amendment for the future, and most humbly ask pardon of God, and Penance and Absolution of you, my Ghostly Father.' Here I finish the *Confiteor:* 'Therefore I beseech the Blessed Mary ever Virgin,' etc.

677. What should we do then?

We should then listen to the advice of the Confessor and be attentive to the penance given us, and should answer his questions with sincerity and humility.

Take care not to leave the confessional until the Priest gives you some sign to go.

§ 5. Satisfaction.

678. What is Satisfaction in the Sacrament of Penance?

Satisfaction is the performance of the Penance given us by the Confessor.

679. Why does the Confessor give us a penance?

He gives us a penance, 1. That we may satisfy for the temporal punishment of our sins; and 2. For the amendment of our life.

680. Does not God remit the punishment of sin when He forgives the sin itself?

He remits the eternal punishment of the sin, but not always the temporal punishment.

681. What is the temporal punishment of our sins?

The temporal punishment of our sins is that punishment which we must suffer either here on earth or afterwards in Purgatory.

682. Is the Confession valid if the penance is not performed?

If after Confession one should fail to perform the penance which in Confession he was willing and intended to perform, the Confession is not rendered invalid, but he commits a new sin and deprives himself of many graces.

683. Should we perform only the penance given us by the Confessor?

We should endeavor to satisfy the Divine Justice by other voluntary works of penance and by patience in our sufferings.

684. What may we expect if we do not make satisfaction?

We may expect to suffer the more in Purgatory.

685. What else must we do after Confession?

After Confession we must, 1. Repair, as well as we can, all injury that we have caused our neighbor; and 2. Use the necessary means to amend our lives and avoid relapsing into sin.

'Sin no more, lest some worse thing happen to thee' (John v. 14).

Application: When you have sinned go at once to Confession, but not without a strict Examination of Conscience, a true Contrition, a firm Purpose of Amendment, and a sincere declaration of your sins, so that this Sacrament of Penance, so rich in grace if properly approached, may not become a cause of eternal perdition for you.

* INDULGENCES.

686. How does the Church help us to discharge the temporal punishment of our sins?

By granting us Indulgences.

687. What is an *Indulgence?*

An Indulgence is a remission of the temporal punishment of our sins which the Church grants us outside the Sacrament of Penance.

688. How can the Church remit the punishment of our sins?

The Church satisfies the Divine Justice out of the great treasure of the merits of Christ and His Saints.

689. What must we believe as to Indulgences?

We must believe, 1. That the Church has power to grant Indulgences; and 2. That the use of them is wholesome.

690. From whom has the Church power to grant Indulgences?

From Jesus Christ, who made no exceptions when He said: 'Whatsoever thou shalt loose on earth, it shall be loosed also in Heaven' (Matt. xvi. 19).

691. What is necessary to gain an Indulgence?

It is necessary, 1. To be in the state of grace; and 2. To perform the good works prescribed for the Indulgence.

692. How many kinds of Indulgences are there?
There are two kinds: *Plenary* Indulgences, which remit all the punishment of sin; and *Partial* Indulgences, which remit only a part of it.

693. Can Indulgences be made of use to the souls in Purgatory?
Yes, all Indulgences which the Pope has indicated for that purpose.

Application: Value Indulgences, and miss no opportunity of gaining them for yourself and for the souls of the faithful departed.

Extreme Unction.

694. What is Extreme Unction?
Extreme Unction is a Sacrament in which a sick person, through the anointing with holy oil, and through the prayer of the Priest, receives the grace of God for the good of the soul, and often also of the body.

The Apostle St. James says of this Sacrament (v. 14, 15): 'Is any man sick among you, let him bring in the Priests of the Church. and let them pray over him, anointing him with oil in the name of the Lord: and the prayer of faith shall save the sick man, and the Lord shall raise him up, and, if he be in sins, they shall be forgiven him.'

695. How is Extreme Unction administered?
The Priest anoints the different senses with holy oil, and at each anointing prays in this form: 'Through this holy unction, and His most tender mercy, may the Lord forgive thee whatever sins thou hast committed by thy *sight*' (by thy *hearing*, etc.)

696. How does Extreme Unction act upon the soul?
Extreme Unction, 1. Increases sanctifying grace; 2. It remits venial sins, and also the mortal sins

which the sick person is no longer able to confess; 3. It takes away the *remains* of sins already forgiven; and 4. It strengthens the soul in its sufferings and temptations, and especially in the struggle of death.

697. How does Extreme Unction act upon the body?

It often relieves the pains of the sick person, and sometimes even restores his health, if recovery be useful for the salvation of his soul.

698. Who can and ought to receive Extreme Unction?

Every Catholic who has come to the use of reason and is in danger of death by sickness.

*699. How should we receive Extreme Unction?

We should receive it, 1. In the state of grace; and we ought, therefore, previously to confess our sins if possible, or at least make an act of perfect contrition; and 2. With faith, hope, charity, and resignation to the will of God.

*700. When should we receive Extreme Unction?

We should receive it, if possible, before we have lost our senses and after having received the Viaticum.

*701. How often can Extreme Unction be received?

As often as we are dangerously ill, and in each illness but once. But we may receive it again upon relapse into danger.

Application: When God in His mercy visits you with a dangerous illness, be careful not to put off receiving the Holy Sacraments to the last moment, lest death surprise you when it is no longer possible to have the attendance of a priest.

*Holy Orders.

702. Upon whom did Christ confer the Priesthood?

Upon His Apostles.

703. Was the Priesthood to end with the death of the Apostles?

No; for the Church was not to end with their death.

704. How has the Priesthood been continued?

The Priesthood has been continued by the Sacrament of Holy Orders.

705. What is the Sacrament of Holy Orders?

Holy Orders is a Sacrament in which the full power of the Priesthood is conferred, as well as a special grace to perform its sacred duties.

706. What are the chief powers of the Priesthood?

The chief powers are, 1. The changing of bread and wine into the Body and Blood of our Lord; and 2. The forgiveness of sins.

707. Who can validly administer this Sacrament?

Bishops, who have received this power by a particular consecration, and none others.

708. What are the visible signs of this Sacrament?

The visible signs are the laying-on of hands, the prayer of the Bishop, the delivery of the chalice with wine, and of the paten with bread.

> By prayer and the laying-on of hands Paul and Barnabas were also ordained : 'Then they, fasting and praying, and imposing their hands upon them, sent them away' (Acts xiii. 3).

709. Can civil authorities or Christian communities confer spiritual powers?

No; they cannot confer spiritual powers on others, for they do not possess them themselves.

710. Can a priest lose his ordination?

No; for, like Baptism, it imprints an indelible mark on the soul.

711. Are there other orders besides those of Priest and Bishop?

There are others, which are preparatory degrees to the Priesthood.

712. Who can and should become Priests?

Only those whom God has called.

Application: Always pay proper respect and submission to Priests, as the representatives of God and the dispensers of His Holy Mysteries, and often pray 'the Lord of the harvest, that He send forth laborers into His harvest' (Matt. ix. 38).

* MATRIMONY.

713. What is the Sacrament of Matrimony?

Matrimony is that Sacrament in which a single man and a single woman are joined together in marriage, and receive grace from God to fulfil the duties of their state faithfully until death.

714. When was Matrimony established?

God established Matrimony in the Garden of Paradise, but Christ raised it to a Sacrament, and the Church has always so believed and taught.

'This is a great Sacrament, but I speak in Christ and in the Church' (Ephes. v. 32).

715. How is this Sacrament received?

The bridegroom and the bride should declare before their Pastor and two witnesses that they take one another as husband and wife, whereupon the Priest blesses their union.

716. What are the duties of married people?

Married people, 1. Should live together in peace, love, and conjugal fidelity until separated by death; 2. They should together bring up their children in the fear of God; and 3. The husband should support and cherish his wife, and the wife should obey her husband in all that is just and honorable.

'Wives, be submissive to your husbands, as it behoveth in the Lord. Husbands, love your wives, and be not bitter towards them ' (Colos. iii. 18, 19).

717. What ought those to remember who think of marrying?

They should remember, 1. Not to make an engagement thoughtlessly; 2. To be properly instructed and free from impediments; 3. To live innocently during the time of their courtship and betrothal; 4. To enter the wedded state with a pure and holy intention; and 5. Before the marriage to make a good Confession and worthily receive Holy Communion.

'We are the children of Saints, and we must not be joined together like heathens that know not God' (Tob. viii. 5).

718. Is it a sin to break a promise of marriage?

Yes; it is a grievous sin, unless the other party agrees, or some just cause requires it to be done.

719. How many kinds of *Impediments* to marriage are there?

There are two kinds of impediments: 1. Such as render marriage *unlawful*, as the forbidden times, the simple vow of chastity, a promise of marriage to another, etc.; and 2. Such as render it *null*, or of no effect, as consanguinity and affinity to the fourth degree inclusive, spiritual relationship, one of the parties not being baptized.

720. What is understood by the *forbidden times?*

The times from the first Sunday of Advent to the Epiphany, and from Ash-Wednesday to Low Sunday, all inclusive, during which times of penance the *solemnizing of marriage* is forbidden by the Church.

721. What of mixed marriages?

The Church has always disapproved of mixed marriages, and permits them only on certain conditions.

Application: When choosing a state of life consult above all things God and the salvation of your soul. If after serious thought you believe yourself called to the married state, prepare for it by prayer, good works, and especially by a good general Confession, and shun the example of those who, by sin and vice, draw the curse of God upon their marriage.

*Sacramentals.

722. What do we usually understand by *Sacramentals*?

By Sacramentals we understand, 1. All those things which the Church blesses, as Holy Water, Oil, Salt, Bread, Wine, Palms, Altars, Chalices, etc.; and 2. The ceremonies of Exorcism and Blessing used by the Church.

723. Why are such things called Sacramentals?

They are called Sacramentals because they resemble the Sacraments, though essentially different from them.

724. Who instituted the Sacramentals?

The Catholic Church instituted the Sacramentals by virtue of the power which Christ gave her to bless, to consecrate, and to exorcise.

725. Why should we make a devout use of Sacramentals?

Because through them we have a part in the prayer and blessing of the universal Church, in whose name the Priest blesses and consecrates.

726. Has the prayer of the Church a particular power?

The prayer of the Church has a particular power, because it is united to the prayer of Jesus and His Saints.

727. What does the Church usually pray for when she consecrates or blesses?

She prays for the turning away of God's judgments, for protection from the devil, for peace, for blessings, and for the welfare of soul and of body.

728. How should we use Holy Water?
A pious Christian sprinkles himself with Holy Water in his house as well as in the church, and at the same time prays God that, through the Blood of Christ, he may be made pure and be saved from all danger.

Application: Use everything which the Church has blessed, and especially Holy Water, with great respect and devotion.

Prayer.

729. What is Prayer?
Prayer is the raising of our hearts to God to praise Him, to thank Him, or to beg His grace; wherefore we speak of Prayer of *Praise*, Prayer of *Thanksgiving*, and Prayer of *Petition*.

730. Is Prayer necessary to all?
Prayer is necessary for salvation to all who have the use of reason.

731. What are the principal fruits of Prayer?
Prayer, 1. Unites us to God and raises our minds to Heaven; 2. Strengthens us against evil, and nerves us to do good; 3. Brings us comfort when in trouble, help when in need, and the grace of perseverance unto death.

732. How must we pray in order to obtain these fruits?
We must pray, 1. With devotion; 2. With humility; 3. With confidence; 4. With resignation to God's will; and 5. With perseverance.

733. When do we pray *with devotion?*
When we pray from the heart, and avoid all distracting thoughts as well as we can.

'This people honoreth me with their lips, but their heart is far from me' (Matt. xv. 8).

734. How may we guard against distraction in Prayer?
Before our Prayers we should free our mind from all worldly thoughts and try to feel ourselves in the presence of God.

'Before Prayer prepare thy soul, and be not as a man that tempteth God' (Ecclus. xviii. 23).

735. When do we pray *with humility*?
When we pray with a clear sense of our weakness and unworthiness.

'The Prayer of him that humbleth himself shall pierce the clouds' (Ecclus. xxxv. 21).
Example: The Pharisee and the Publican (Luke xviii.)

736. When do we pray with confidence?
When we firmly hope that God will hear our prayer, so far as it tends to His honor and to our salvation.

'This is that trust, which we have in Him, that He hearkens to all that we ask according to His will' (1 John v. 14).

737. Why ought we to have this firm hope?
Because God can grant us all good things, and for the sake of Jesus will do so.

'Amen, amen, I say to you, if you ask the Father anything in my name, He will give it to you' (John xvi. 23; comp. Mark xi. 23, 24).

738. But why do we not always receive what we pray for?
1. Because we do not pray as we ought; or 2. Because we ask for what would not be good for our salvation; or 3. Because we do not persevere in praying.

739. When do we pray with resignation to God's will?

When we leave entirely to God how and when He will grant what we ask in our prayer.

'Father, not my will, but Thine be done' (Luke xxii. 42).

740. When do we pray with perseverance?
When we continue to pray all the more earnestly although our prayer seems not to be heard.

Examples: The woman of Chanaan (Matt. xv.); parable of the friend who asks for three loaves (Luke xi. 5–10).

741. Must we always pray in a set form of words?
No; we do this in Oral Prayer only; we can also use Interior Prayer, or Meditation.

742. What is Meditation?
Meditation is reflection upon the life and sufferings of our Saviour, or upon the other truths of religion, in order to excite in our hearts pious sentiments and especially good resolutions.

743. When ought we to pray?
Christ says 'we ought always to pray, and not to faint' (Luke xviii. 1).

744. How can we pray always?
We pray always when we often raise our hearts to God, and offer Him all our work, sufferings, and pleasures. Yet at certain times we must pray in a particular manner.

745. When must we pray in a particular manner?
1. In times of temptation, need, or calamity; 2. Morning and night; before and after meals; at the Angelus; and when in church.

746. For whom must we pray?
We must pray for all men.

Application: Consider what a privilege it is that you, who are a miserable worm of the earth, may converse with the Most High God as a child does with his father.

Pray often, therefore, with as much devotion as you can, whether at home or in church. 'Ask, and it shall be given you; seek, and you shall find; knock, and it shall be opened to you' (Luke xi. 9).

§ 1. *The Lord's Prayer.*

747. Which is the most excellent Prayer?
The most excellent Prayer is the Our Father, or Lord's Prayer.

748. Why is the Our Father called the Lord's Prayer?
Because Christ our Lord taught it to us and commanded us to say it (Matt. vi. 9–13).

Say the Lord's Prayer ('Our Father,' etc., see page 5).

749. What does the Lord's Prayer contain?
It contains a Preface and Seven Petitions.

750. Which is the Preface?
'Our Father who art in Heaven.'

751. What does the word Father remind us of?
That God is our Father, and that we ought to pray to Him with child-like reverence, love, and confidence.

752. Why do we say *our* Father, and not *my* Father?
Because God is the Father of *all* men, and we must, therefore, pray for one another as brethren.

753. Why do we add: '*Who art in Heaven*'?
To remind ourselves that when we pray we must take our heart away from earthly things and raise it to Heaven.

754. What do we ask in the *First* Petition: '*Hallowed be Thy name*'?
In the first Petition we ask that God's name may not be profaned or blasphemed, and that He may be better known and honored.

755. What do we ask in the *Second* Petition: '*Thy Kingdom come*'?

In the second petition we ask, 1. That the kingdom of God, the Church, may increase on earth; 2. That the kingdom of Divine Grace and Love may be established in our hearts; and 3. That we may be all admitted into the kingdom of Heaven.

756. What do we ask in the *Third* Petition: ' *Thy will be done on earth as it is in Heaven* ' ?

In the Third Petition we ask that we and all men may do the will of God on earth as the Angels and Saints do it in Heaven.

757. What do we ask in the *Fourth* Petition: ' *Give us this day our daily bread* ' ?

In the Fourth Petition we ask God to give us what we daily need for soul and body.

758. What do we ask in the *Fifth* Petition: ' *Forgive us our trespasses, as we forgive them that trespass against us* ' ?

In the Fifth Petition we ask God to forgive us all our sins, as we forgive all who have offended us.

759. What do we ask in the *Sixth* Petition: ' *Lead us not into temptation* ' ?

In the Sixth Petition we ask that God will withdraw all temptations and dangers from us, or at least give us the grace to overcome them.

760. Why does God let us be tempted?

1. To make us humble and watchful; and 2. To increase our merit and our zeal for virtue.

761. What must we do to overcome temptation?

We must watch and pray, for Christ our Lord says. ' Watch ye and pray that ye enter not into temptation ' (Matt. xxvi. 41).

762. What do we ask in the *Seventh* Petition: ' *But deliver us from evil* ' ?

In the Seventh Petition we ask that God will preserve us from all ill of soul or body, and especially from sin and eternal damnation.

763. Why do we add ' Amen ' ?

Because 'Amen,' or 'So be it,' expresses our earnest desire and our confidence of being heard.

Application: Always say the Lord's Prayer with great respect and attention, for it is the prayer which our Divine Redeemer Himself has taught us.

§ 2. *The Angelical Salutation.*

764. What prayer is, next to the Lord's Prayer, the most familiar?
The prayer in honor of the Mother of God, called the *Angelical Salutation, Hail Mary,* or *Ave Maria.*

765. How many parts has the Hail Mary?
Two parts, a *Prayer of Praise* and a *Prayer of Petition.*

766. What constitutes the *Prayer of Praise?*
1. The words of the Archangel Gabriel: '*Hail [Mary], full of grace, the Lord is with thee; blessed art thou among women*'; and 2. The words of St. Elizabeth: '*And blessed is the fruit of thy womb,*' to which we add the name of *Jesus.* (*Hail* means '*Be well,*' '*Health to thee,*' or '*I salute thee*'; in Latin '*Ave,*' or '*Salve.*')

767. When were these words spoken?
1. When the Archangel Gabriel announced to the Blessed Virgin Mary that she would become the Mother of God; and 2. When Mary went into the hill-country to visit her cousin Elizabeth.

768. Why do we say, '*Full of grace*'?
1. Because Mary was filled with grace, even before her birth; 2. Because she grew in grace; and 3. Because she brought forth the Author of all grace.

769. Why do we say, '*the Lord is with thee*'?
Because the ever-blessed Virgin Mary was most closely united with God on earth, and is now, as

Queen of Saints, next to the Throne of God in Heaven.

770. Why do we say, '*Blessed art thou among women*'?

We say so to praise Mary, who was chosen from amongst all virgins to be the Mother of God.

771. Why do we add, '*Blessed is the fruit of thy womb, Jesus*'?

To show that the veneration of Mary and the veneration of Christ are inseparable, and that we praise the Mother for the sake of her Son.

772. What make the Prayer of Petition?

The words added by the Church: '*Holy Mary, Mother of God, pray for us sinners, now, and at the hour of our death. Amen.*'

773. Why did the Church add these words?

So that we may often beg the intercession of the ever-blessed Virgin Mary in all our needs, and especially that we may obtain through her the grace of a happy death.

774. What is the '*Angelus*'?

It is a prayer which we say morning, noon, and night in honor of the *Incarnation*.

775. How do we say the '*Angelus*'?

'The Angel of the Lord,' etc. (See page 9.)

Application: Honor the Blessed Virgin in a most particular and childlike manner. Ask her help in all needs and troubles, and try to imitate her charity, patience, purity, and other virtues.

RELIGIOUS PRACTICES AND CEREMONIES.

776. What is meant by *Religious Ceremonies*?

Religious Ceremonies are signs and actions full of meaning which the Church has established for Divine Service.

777. But are not Ceremonies empty and idle observances?

Certainly not: for, 1. God Himself prescribed several kinds of ceremonies to the Jews under severe penalties; Christ our Lord used ceremonies; and 3. He himself instituted Sacramental signs or Ceremonies.

778. Have all Religious Ceremonies a meaning?

Yes; everything used by the Church in Divine Service has a mystical meaning and is intended to excite us to devotion.

779. What is the meaning of *Incense?*

Incense is an emblem of reverence and prayer which ascends to Heaven as a sweet odor before God (Ps. cxl. 2).

780. What is the meaning of *Lighted Candles?*

Lighted Candles signify Faith, which enlightens, Hope, which soars above this world, and Charity, which sets our hearts on fire; and they remind us, also, of the times of persecution, when Christians were obliged to worship in underground caverns.

781. What is the meaning of the *Paschal Candle?*

The Paschal Candle reminds us of Jesus Christ, who arose from the dead, rescued us from the slavery of Satan, and is a light to us, as was the *pillar of fire* to the Jews who escaped the bondage of Egypt (Exod. xiv. 20).

782. What is the meaning of the *Ashes* on Ash Wednesday?

The Ashes on Ash Wednesday remind us that we should humble ourselves and repent, and therefore the Priest, in putting ashes upon our heads, says: 'Remember, man, that thou art dust, and unto dust thou shalt return' (Gen. iii. 19).

Ashes were in ancient times also an emblem of penance and humility. *Examples:* The Ninivites, Judith, Esther, etc.

783. What is the meaning of the *Palms* on Palm Sunday?

The Palms remind us of the triumphal entry of our Saviour into Jerusalem, and of His victory over Hell.

784. What is the meaning of *Religious Processions?*

Religious Processions are intended, 1. To make known the Catholic faith before all the world and to proclaim the praise of God; 2. To entreat the blessing of God upon town and country; and 3. To celebrate the triumph of Christianity. And, therefore, the Cross and Banners are displayed.

785. What should we think of Pilgrimages?

When made as the Church desires they are praiseworthy, and they have been so practised by the Saints.

786. How does the Church desire that Pilgrimages should be made?

The Church desires, 1. That we should not neglect our duties for them; 2. That we should have a good intention; 3. That we should well employ the time that we are on the way; and 4. That we should pray fervently at the holy place, and, if possible, receive the Sacraments there.

787. What are Confraternities?

They are pious associations, mostly approved by the Popes, established for mutual prayer, encouragement, and assistance in good works and for frequently receiving the Holy Sacraments.

Application: Take pleasure in assisting devoutly at the Ceremonies of the Church, and do not be hindered by the mockery or example of thoughtless or impious people.

RECAPITULATION.

1. *Our Religion is Divine.*

This is proved by her history from the beginning of the world up to the present time, and is made clear by her age, her Founder, her duration, her blessings, her works, etc.

Our Divine Religion teaches us that we have been created in order that we may serve God in this life, and be eternally happy with Him in the next.

For this end we must, 1. Believe all that God has revealed (pages 51–56); 2. Keep all the Commandments which God has given us Himself (pages 92–115) or through His Church (pages 115–120); consequently, avoid sin by which the Commandments are broken (pages 120–125), and strive to lead a virtuous life (pages 125-130); but to do this we must have the Grace of God (pages 131–133). Therefore we must also, 3. Make use of the Means of Grace which God has ordained, which are the Sacraments (pages 134–167) and Prayer (pages 168–174).

www.ingramcontent.com/pod-product-compliance
Lightning Source LLC
Chambersburg PA
CBHW020255170426
43202CB00008B/388